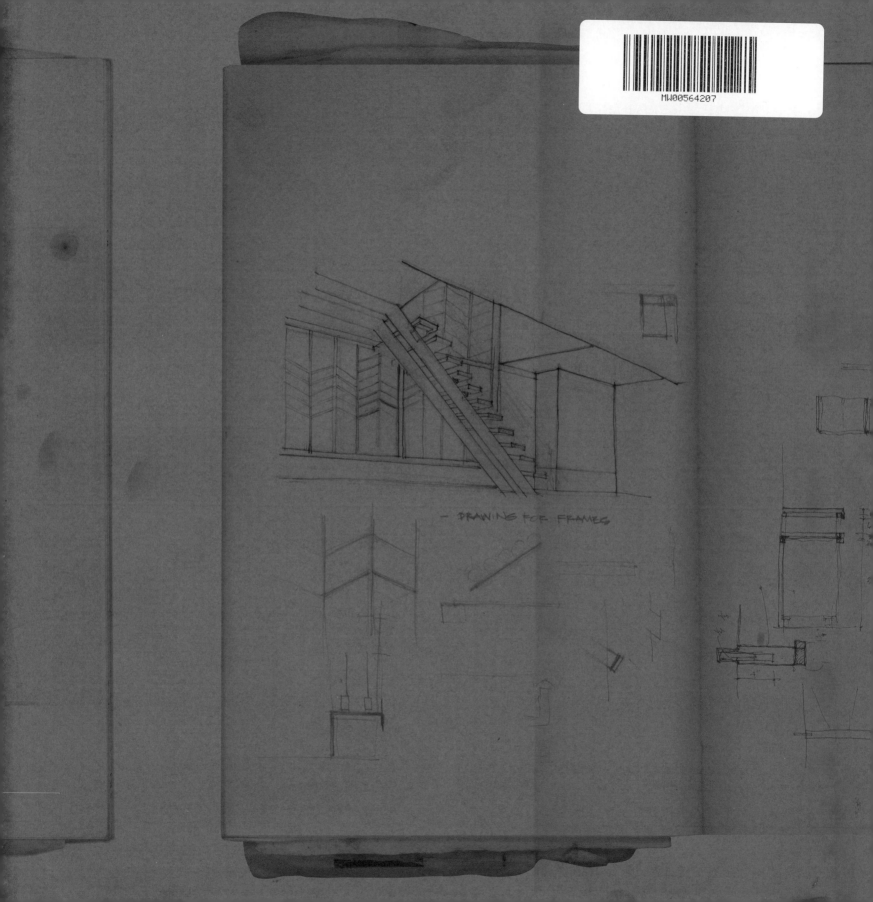

— DRAWING FOR FRAMES

BEST
UGLY

RESTAURANT
CONCEPTS
AND
ARCHITECTURE
BY AVROKO

COLLINS | DESIGN

An Imprint of HarperCollinsPublishers

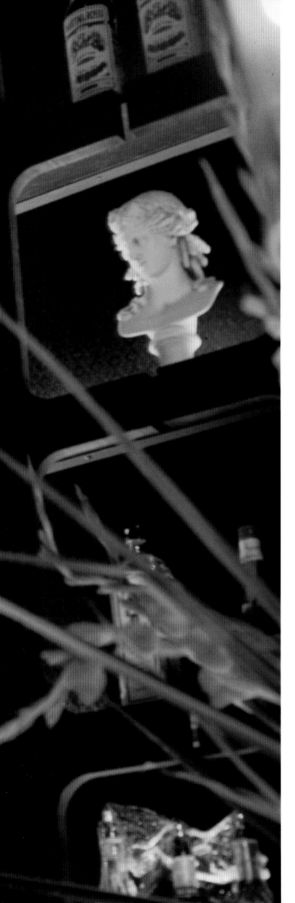

PHOTOGRAPHY CREDITS

Yuki Kuwana: pages ii, 6, 8, 18, 19, 20, 23, 24, 26, 28, 29, 30, 32, 35, 36, 37, 40, 41, 44, 45, 47, 48, 50, 60, 61, 62, 64, 70, 73, 78, 81, 86, 89, 90, 92, 100, 102, 104, 107, 108, 112, 113, 114, 117, 118, 122, 124, 125, 127, 128, 129, 130, 140, 141, 142, 144, 146, 150, 153, 154, 155, 156, 158, 161, 162, 164, 165, 166, 167, 168, 170, 180, 184, 185, 186, 188, 189, 192, 194, 196, 198, 200, 202, 209, 212, 216, 218, 220, 222, 224, 227, 228, 232, 234, 235, 238, 239, 244, 245.

Michael Weber: pages iv, vi, 21, 22, 25, 31, 34, 38, 42, 43, 62, 65, 68, 73, 77, 79, 80, 83, 87, 106, 110, 123, 142, 143, 145, 148, 149, 151, 152, 157, 159, 160, 182, 191, 193, 195, 197, 214, 217, 219, 221, 225, 226, 229, 230, 231, 233, 234, 236, 237.

Michael Kleinberg: pages 103, 105, 106, 109, 111, 115, 119, 120.

Paul Guba: pages 28, 46, 199.

Raymond Patrick: page 3.

Jordan Provost: page 39.

Travis Schnupp: page 67.

Additional Credits: Division of Rare and Manuscript Collections, Cornell University Library, page 20. Berenice Abbott; page 66. Museum of the City of New York, The Byron Collection; page 69. Collection of the Kyoto Costume Institute, photos by Kazumi Kurigami(Kimono) and Takashi Hatakeyama(Corset); page 76. Collection of the Kyoto Costume Institute, photo by Takashi Hatakeyama; page 82. Science, Industry & Business Library, The New York Public Library, Astor, Lenox and Tilden Foundations; page 150. Niche Modern; page 160. National Museum and Gallery of Wales, Cardiff, UK / Bridgeman Art Library; page 173. Washington University Libraries, Deptartment of Special Collections; page 184. Christie's Images Ltd.; page 190. Thos. Hunter, Lith. Philadelphia; page 215. Shuli Sade; page 232. Getty Images; pages 11, 16, 21, 58, 59, 62, 63, 95, 116, 133, 138, 178, 185, 205, 210, 218. Corbis Images; pages 53, 88, 107, 121, 126.

HarperCollins books may be purchased for educational, business, or sales promotional use. For information please write: Special Markets Department, HarperCollins Publishers, 10 East 53rd Street, New York, NY 10022.

FIRST EDITION

Designed by AvroKO

Library of Congress Cataloging-in-Publication Data has been applied for.

ISBN 10: 0-06-113693-X

ISBN 13: 978-0-06-113693-1

07 08 09 10 11 10 9 8 7 6 5 4 3 2 1

TO OUR PARENTS

for the tremendous examples they have set, the considerable support they have provided, and the unconditional love they have shown us over the years.

TABLE OF CONTENTS

A REMARKABLE LACK OF DISCIPLINE

JON CRAWFORD-PHILLIPS

This book is not just about design, and it's certainly not just about great restaurants. It's about a unique approach to design that goes beyond, or rather before, a fascination with function or a celebration of the aesthetic. It's about creating a meaningful experience for the visitor—an experience that makes us think, feel, remember, and understand. It's what AvroKO calls Design Connectivity.

Founded by four principals (Greg Bradshaw, Adam Farmerie, Kristina O'Neal, and William Harris), AvroKO was established as a design and concept firm. And while they do great design, it is their collective obsession with meaning—with bringing to life a concept—that sets them apart. And it's probably why you're reading this book. Design, for AvroKO, is a means to an end, and so integration, in this case, is not about the integration of new media into design strategy or of multiple disciplines into one company. It's about the integration of a psychologically connected concept with an ergonomic and aesthetic vision, even before design begins.

You only have to spend time with AvroKO during the first few weeks of a project to understand the role of connectivity in their design process. They research more than just materials, fittings, and furniture because they're not just building a visual theme or a workable space—they're building a connected and meaningful experience. They research every cultural nuance and social context until they reach a thorough understanding of the psychological concept of a project. And they do this long, long before they start thinking about walnut paneling and cold-rolled steel.

Context is woven into AvroKO's restaurant experiences as fundamentally as texture, color, and light. And this context—whether it is the co-existence of French and Vietnamese provincial aesthetics in Sapa, the nostalgia of urban municipality in PUBLIC, or The Stanton Social's celebration of deconstructed vintage fashion—is not just a fascination with eclectic design trends. It's meaningful, consid-ered, obsessive, and it gives rise to a powerful experience with deep integrity. AvroKO doesn't do themed design, and they don't do obvious design. Their restaurants engage your senses. They make you think and make you realize the value of being made to think. They put the experience not just in the eye, but also in the mind of the beholder.

AvroKO's process is as simple as it is elegant, which explains how the four principals of the design team can agree so consistently and coherently on a given project. They focus their individual sub-jectivities on the definition of a singular yet multi-faceted concept, and subsequently on the execution of that concept through design. This framework liberates AvroKO from the pressures of pursuing the next new look or uniqueness for uniqueness's sake. You don't have to design your way to an idea if the idea is already there; design is the means by which that idea is manifest in the physical, psychologi-cal, and emotional world.

Which leads me to the slightly inflammatory title for this introduc-tion: Without doubt the most unique quality about AvroKO is their remarkable lack of discipline. They are, in the truest sense of the word, design-agnostic. They create connected experiences—psycho-logically, ergonomically, and aesthetically—and they do this better than anyone I know. Incorporating interior design, structural design, graphic design, furniture design, culinary design, interactive design, and any other kind of design that enters the picture, they know how to hit upon a great concept and bring it fully to life—and nowhere is this more evident than in the restaurants featured in this book.

AvroKO define themselves by the concept they conceive, the experience they create, and the meaning they inspire in those who inhabit their spaces. Design is what they do along the way, with an unswerving faith in their idea and a conscientious lack of discipline. That's remarkable.

"You don't have to design your way to an idea if the idea is already there; design is the means by which that idea is manifest in the physical, psychological, and emotional world."

A FIRESIDE CHAT WITH THE PRINCIPALS OF AVROKO

INTERVIEWER: JON CRAWFORD-PHILLIPS **(JCP)**
AVROKO: GREG BRADSHAW **(GB)**, ADAM FARMERIE **(AF)**, KRISTINA O'NEAL **(KO)**, WILLIAM HARRIS **(WH)**

[OFF MIC COMMENTS] [LAUGHTER]

JCP: Okay, what is AvroKO?

WH: AvroKO is essentially a merger of two companies. Adam and Greg had an architecture firm called Avro Design. And Kristina and I had a company called KO Media Studios, which did design and concept work. In the late nineties we started to collaborate on projects and found a...how do you say it–

AF: –I believe we said synergy.

[LAUGHTER]

WH: Ummmm yeah, it was a collaboration, and we just sort of had a synergy amongst the four of us, the way in which we worked, and so we started working together more and more often. Eventually we decided to make it official.

JCP: Was there a moment when you realized that this was actually something, other than that you had fun together, that this was–

AF: –The real deal.

JCP: Yeah, worth bringing all these random bits together?

AF: I don't think there was a moment at all. I think that's what made it so seamless. It was just eventually becoming one company, and it actually started a long, long, time ago, when we all went to school together.

KO: That is an interesting point that I don't think we have talked about very often, but that we literally started collaborating at 18.

WH: Yeah, we were collaborating on each others' projects and helping each other out, all the way back when. So, when we started doing it professionally it seemed very natural. And there was never a point where we said, "Oh, well, we should really kind of do this for a living, we should combine these companies."

GB: We just eventually melded into each other, working on more projects together. And eventually it just became—we became, one company.

JCP: Okay, so when you finally made it official, what did you see AvroKO becoming? Did you have a business plan?

KO: From the time that we first started coming together, we weren't vehicle specific. We were feeling that anything could happen in terms of the types of design we could do. But Greg said, there is no way we're not going to do architecture, and back then it really was feasible that we could end up not doing architecture at all.

AF: I think what ended up happening is that it became immediately evident that there were a number of different things that each of us wanted to do. There wasn't a corporate model that we could point to and say, this is the type of format that we should follow, and that's the kind of client we'll go after, and that's the kind of design we'll do. It just

became, "What do you personally enjoy... What are your passions?"

JCP: And how has that evolved over the years?

AF: The beauty of the beginning of this...we should talk a little bit about this, because I think the catalyst to a lot of this was what we called Kristina's Magic Paper, what *she* called the Magic Paper, which basically was a system of questions getting to the heart of everyone's hopes, desires and dreams. I think we all realized that we were just not inspired by other models that were out there and not really interested in necessarily being completely pigeonholed or having a long track of expected milestones ahead of us. I think the adventure and the excitement was what fueled a lot of this, so–

WH: –That's also what led us to deciding that it was okay to allow ourselves to deviate from doing client work. We thought, "It's fine to do a restaurant, it's fine to explore a sort of urban living conundrum, through our Smart Space condos. It's fine to do furniture." We just get to create and be happy.

[OVERTALK]

AF: Well, it becomes Magic Paper.

WH: If that's the heart of what makes you happy and you're into it–

GB: –You have to do it.

JCP: So where did the focus on restaurants come from?

AvroKO principals from left to right:
Greg Bradshaw, Adam Farmerie, Kristina O'Neal, William M...

AF: Well, we think restaurants are interesting animals. They have all of the interesting psychological design elements, while still maintaining artistic features that are grounded in architecture, as well as graphics, as well as diving into food and more tertiary things like music, uniforms, etc. You can just completely engulf yourself in the experience. It becomes a harmony of all of these different mediums coming together.

KO: It's really one of the few design vehicles that encompasses that many different artistic pursuits, and we try do it in such a balance that it develops into a complete experience.

WH: It definitely encompasses not only the artistic pursuits, but the lifestyle pursuits as well. And that's a great interest of ours–good living and food and wine and sociability.

JCP: How do you guys bring together your differing skills—or is every restaurant project done by a different person?

KO: William and I have a certain skill set, and Greg and Adam have a certain skill set, in terms of the way we're processing information and translating it into concrete design or concept work. And the restaurants are really a perfect canvas for dealing with the fact that we're coming from two different places and bringing them together, conceptually and pragmatically–

AF: –And maybe there's even more than two.

KO: Oh, yeah, certainly it gets more diversified than that, significantly more diversified once we get into details.

WH: Well, I think that we have developed something unique, in that there is a difference between the way maybe somebody thinks who is trained as an architect versus somebody who is trained as an artist. Our approach, in any project, allows for those two slightly divergent points of view to participate equally.

JCP: Okay. So looking at the next five years. Is there a focus for the next five years?

KO: We still have things on our to-do lists. It seems there is a lot we haven't achieved.

GB: You know, it's still a process. I think it's also just to keep moving it to the next level. We haven't gotten into any more structural architecture yet and we would like to. It's a whole other exercise to deal with an entire building from the outside-in, through all the varying levels.

WH: There is also a natural growth that has come out of our interests and we hope to keep growing in directions that encompass a whole lifestyle, it grows from restaurants to literal living spaces, which becomes very hospitality based. So we're getting much more involved in hotel work and other living spaces that have all these elements combined.

KO: A fully integrated approach.

WH: The whole integrated approach, yeah. I think hotels are definitely becoming a large part of our future.

JCP: People talk about how you kind of have a respect—when you design a restaurant you have a respect for what's already there and the kind of structural fabric that already exists. How does that apply to your New York restaurant design?

AF: That's just because we don't have any budgets to work with.

[LAUGHTER] [OVERTALK] [LAUGHTER]

KO: It's been very true of the New York restaurant work. If people knew what kind of small budgets we had to design with for these first restaurants, they might feel a bit amused. And I think that trying to break into architecture is hard enough, but when people came to us with these budgets, we were using as much ingenuity as we could possibly muster, and you can't–

AF: –You can only stretch the thing so many ways.

[OVERTALK]

GB: But you've got to use what you can from the pre-existing space. And I think a lot of our design style has developed out of those early parameters. It's an industrial style and we count on as much preservation of the history of the building as possible in the New York restaurants...but frankly it's also been cost effective.

AF: It's all true. At the end of the day when you don't have a budget, you have fewer choices.

GB: Yeah, but we love that stuff anyway—a weathered wall or a wood beamed ceiling that is already existing is usually something to celebrate rather than cover up. We are attracted to buildings with some natural character.

WH: If there's anything that is extremely consistent and is also one of the things I'm happiest about, it's that we try to maintain a sense of structural honesty in the New York restaurant work.

GB: But it comes down to, even if you've got a white box, and it is all about drywall, that's okay. Our philosophy stays the same...try to stay honest to the space. We just have to change our techniques about how we treat the different variables in the space. It's still an honest approach. A developer may have built a space this way because it was the cheapest way to do it. We just ask ourselves, how are we going to work within those limitations?

JCP: Talk about what you all mean when you say, "honest."

GB: It's about letting people know how something is built and trying not to fake anything. Typically you don't put up a faux brick wall, you know? However, it might be okay to put up a faux brick wall, but then reveal some aspect of it that tells people, oh, that is intentionally a faux brick wall, and I can actually see the studs popping up at the top there. And it adds a sense of layering to it, and it shows people how things are actually built.

JCP: The honesty then, how does that apply to a concept?

WH: We're never interested in just recreating something from another time period or geographic location to support a concept—that feels too forced.

KO: There's more juxtaposition, and there's more interest on our part in developing something new from real references—it taps into the underbelly of a concept, not the top. I mean you have to go several layers deep and then several steps sideways with a concept and that's where the honesty is located.

AF: I think that's also what leads to our obsession with history. Often we do go back to things in history that had a certain honesty to them. You know, certain trades or ways in which people work with materials, or particular areas of New York, for example, and you go and find the history behind the reference.

JCP: So you have formed a collective creative vision. Is this a challenge?

AF: It is a challenging situation. One that I think works really well though. We all have different perspectives as individuals, certainly. And I think that is exactly what has made the projects stronger and more layered. We all kind of fill different needs here or there.

KO: And we all play off of each other well. So there's definitely a filtering process, and there's a passing on, or a lateral thinking process that happens. But, certainly we have different opinions and there's never one final voice. It's definitely more democratic.

AF: Even though we are somewhat of a creative oligarchy, there are times in the project that require different principals to take the lead. So you don't have, oli-oli-in-come-free.

JCP: Once you agree on an idea then, every production decision is not subject to the four of you?

WH: Once we've got that point of departure, we're saying, here is the direction we have all agreed to go.

JCP: It's a reference point.

KO: Yes it's the reference point. And then you know that the map can't go that far—its drawn out to suit the concept. You know, it's got to be somewhat contained but with plenty of room to move in that contained area.

JCP: It sounds like you guys have worked out your creative process.

KO: Well, beyond working together, we enjoy each other socially, and I think that that enjoyment has actually become part of the creative process— a fairly interesting–

AF: –Synergy.

[LAUGHTER]

WH: –Synergy and oligarchiness.

[LAUGHTER]

GB: Jesus.

[LAUGHTER]

AF: You know...We're never going to write this, but the whole idea of achievement, it's useless to some degree, it's more like the saying "If you do what you love, with people you enjoy, you never work another day in your life" kind of thing, but it's true for us. We are just happy to be here.

DESIGN PRINCIPLE

#01

BEST UGLY

AND OTHER PRINCIPLES OF DESIGN CONNECTIVITY

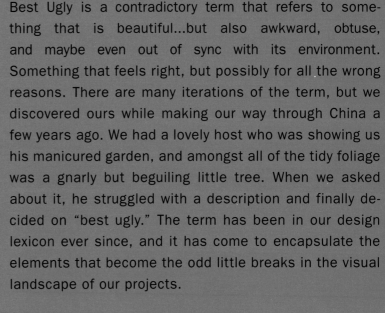

Best Ugly is a contradictory term that refers to something that is beautiful...but also awkward, obtuse, and maybe even out of sync with its environment. Something that feels right, but possibly for all the wrong reasons. There are many iterations of the term, but we discovered ours while making our way through China a few years ago. We had a lovely host who was showing us his manicured garden, and amongst all of the tidy foliage was a gnarly but beguiling little tree. When we asked about it, he struggled with a description and finally decided on "best ugly." The term has been in our design lexicon ever since, and it has come to encapsulate the elements that become the odd little breaks in the visual landscape of our projects.

Best Ugly elements are just one of the features of our design process that can be applied in any medium. Since we are not vehicle specific—meaning we aren't tied to being "architects" even though the majority of our work is thought to be in this arena—we think of our projects as a way to blend several mediums in bringing a concept to life. When pressed to put a label on our process, the closest we have come is "Design Connectivity," as a way to express that every element in an interior should connect or have a relationship with every other element in that interior, as well as to the soul of the concept. This allows viewers to honestly "feel" a space. This connectivity is possibly most present in our New York restaurant work, and this book is both a look at how we have developed that process as well as the environments that have resulted.

PUBLIC

THE TOTAL SOCIETY

KRISTI CAMERON

If any one project represents the full richness of AvroKO's Integrated Design approach, it is PUBLIC. Tucked behind a deceptively workaday staircase in Manhattan's boutique NoLIta neighborhood, this singular restaurant unites diverse design elements as effortlessly as its eclectic menu melds myriad inspirations. PUBLIC is also exceptional because the firm actually owns and operates the eatery in partnership with chef Brad Farmerie (Adam's brother) and former restaurant consultant Dan Rafalin.

The concept for the design sprang from the quality of the food itself, an international medley of familiar ingredients. A typical entrée, for example, might be roast duck breast made new in combination with bok choy, cassava chips, sesame soy dressing, and pickled chilies. Because the team regards making good food accessible as a public service, they landed on a municipal motif. "We looked back to the last time that public services were revered in American society, which was the '30s and '40s and the WPA projects of that time," Farmerie said. "You could count on the government, you could count on municipal services."

As ingenious as the concept is, government architecture doesn't typically lend itself to a pleasurable dining atmosphere, and so its success lies in the nuanced execution. AvroKO excels at establishing believable working metaphors and then blending the old and the new, the familiar and the surprising, in meticulous detail to realize them. At PUBLIC the feeling of civic nostalgia seizes you as soon as you top those concrete steps and meet a cluster of brass mailboxes sus-

pended out of time. In the reception area you'll find an oak card catalog that holds period titles such as *The Charming Woman* and *The "Have-More" Plan*. At some point you will also notice the backlit pebbled glass doors to the bathrooms, which evoke a noir film or a trip to the principal's office. "We all have a proclivity toward certain historical elements," said Bradshaw, who salvaged the doors. "We reference certain eras—the '20s, '30s, and '40s—because we like them, but also because those structures are getting torn down and there's so much great stuff out there. This is Americana."

And in a way, PUBLIC is Everytown, America. "All towns have a post office and a library, but we didn't want to make it too themed," O'Neal emphasizes. "It wasn't supposed to be a carnival but something you might have memories of, placed in an entirely different form and context." Toward that end, the found objects are interwoven with new elements. Faced with the need to store wine bottles in a sealed space, AvroKO housed them in a glass structure that serves as a second partition for the private dining area. Likewise, AvroKO gave the communal table a clever twist with a custom design of individual tops that slide on an aluminum eyebeam, allowing them to be combined as one long surface.

Though PUBLIC's graphics—the wine lists, menus, and guest checks—look as though they were taken directly from the files of a civil servant, they are inspired originals. Bearing ledger-like markings on a manila background, the materials are printed in simple courier type. The designers hand made each narrow clipboard on which the wine list arrives and

hand stamp every document they print—a gesture not unlike notarization. "I am proud of the menus in particular, because there were a lot of functional dilemmas that we had to solve," Harris said. "The menu changes constantly, from individual ingredients to whole dishes, so we had to come up with a system that allows us to adjust these quickly and print them out. We came up with a perforation device that lets us print two menus at a time. That allowed us to retain this great perforated edge when they're torn, which is very governmental."

That kind of personal touch extends beyond the physical space to the community that PUBLIC has become. For example, guests have consistently donated materials to the library since the restaurant first opened. The mailboxes—conceived for a wine club in which people who rented them would receive bottles selected by the chef—are the best example of the PUBLIC community. Originally inspired by the stein lockers in German beer halls, the program has evolved over time to include theater tickets, music, and homemade orange marmalade.

PUBLIC is a particularly good example of AvroKO's unique Integrated Design approach: "I think that across the board when we were talking about the early concept, materials, and formal design elements, connectivity is what we were hoping for at the end of the day—especially with PUBLIC, because we were our own client," O'Neal said. "We didn't need to filter. We came out of the gate saying 'What if?' and we just did it."

REVEALING HISTORY

The early stages of developing PUBLIC's design were some of the most trying months for the firm. With very little money for the build-out, and approximately four months to design and build a restaurant from the bare bones of a former muffin factory, PUBLIC presented us with our first real opportunity to work formally as a team without any client restrictions. However, we had more than a few moments of scratching our heads at three a.m. in the midst of the construction dust saying, "I am not sure how this one is going to happen."

In spite of all this, we did have a few good things going for us. The building structure was stunning and remarkably spacious. We had the benefit of an unheard-of amount of square footage in a neighborhood notorious for its narrow, 25-foot-wide, 50-foot-deep tenement buildings (we co-joined two neighboring buildings by creating large passageways between them, adding stairs to account for the elevation change, and creating a new opening in the façade of the building to access the 6000 square feet that now exist as PUBLIC). But beyond all of the structural

changes needed to make this space work, what proved to be our greatest asset was our newly formulated integrated design process, which we hadn't put a name to at the time, but would become the foundation upon which we would build all of our subsequent restaurant projects.

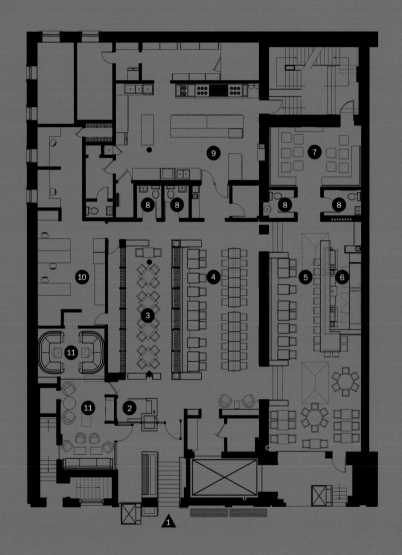

1. ENTRY

2. HOST

3. WINE ROOM

4. UPPER DINING

5. LOWER DINING

6. BAR

7. BACK LOUNGE

8. RESTROOMS

9. KITCHEN

10. OFFICES

11. THE MONDAY ROOM

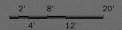

2'   8'   20'

4'   12'

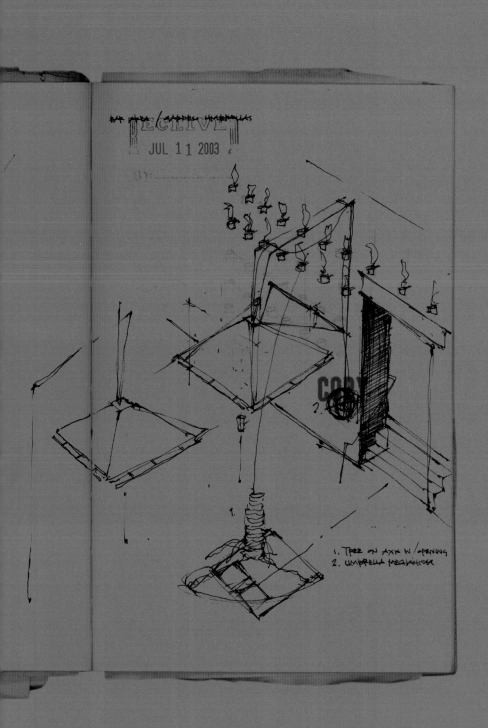

1. TREE ON AXIE W/OPENING
2. UMBRELLA MECHANISM

• ROWS OF AQUARIUS
HAIR DRYER, WALL MOUNTED, PINK

• VATS OF MOUTHWASH
STAINLESS STEEL
DENTIST SPITTING BOWL

STUDY FOR BATHROOMS:

BATH 1: SOUND | EAR PLUGS AND Q-TIPS

BATH 2: SMELL | HOTEL SIZED SOAPS W/ PUBLIC STAMPS, POSS. OPEN STALLED CONT. (SMALL SIZE)

BATH 3: TASTE | HOMAGE TO THE DENTIST, POSS. USING TOOLS FOR HAND TOWELS, DIXIE CUPS W/ MOUTHWASH BOTTLES

BATH 4: VISION | SALON, ROWS AND ROWS OF AQUANET, BLUE LIQUID W/ COMBS, HAIR DRYER, TWENTY MIRRORS OF SHAPE + SIZE

ANECHOIC CHAMBER WALLS?
PIPED IN SOUND OF WATER?

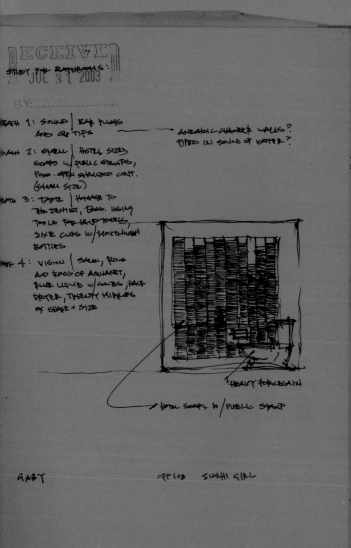

HEAVY PORCELAIN

HOTEL SOAPS W/ PUBLIC STAMP

GARY   OFFICE SUSHI GIRL

PLANNING SESSION W/ ___

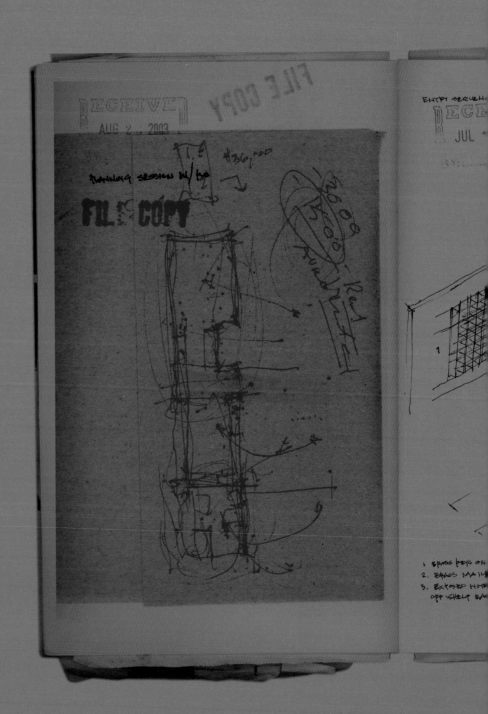

16

KEYSTONE VIEW COMPANY
STUDIOS, MEADVILLE, PA.
COPYRIGHTED

14 22080 Spinning Cotton Yarn in the Great Textile Mills, Lawrence, Mass.

WHY MUNICIPAL?

The name PUBLIC was derived from a desire to suggest that quality food should be a common commodity. In exploring the connection between other public institutions and the goods and services they provide, it seemed that we were potentially treading on thin ice. With government funding cutbacks for the public parks systems, libraries, and schools, the near-abandonment of the NEA, and the potential disappearance of Social Security—on a Guns-and-Butter graph somewhere, publicly provided commodities seemed to be on a downward slope.

However, while sitting around romanticizing the role of governments and communities, and their providence for the Public Good, there seemed a time in recent history where we could look for encouragement. The excesses of the 1920s and the tragedies of the

Great Depression provided fertile ground for social brilliance. FDR-era America seemed to epitomize the ideals of the common commodity for which we were searching. Some of the building projects created at this time, through the Works Progress Administration or otherwise, had the same effect as the medieval European cathedral or mosque had on its constituents—they provided the common man with a belief that there was an institution larger than himself in which he could have faith. Through the scale of these spaces, the solidity of their building materials, and the artistry of their details, people began to believe in the power of the government that was caring for them. In attempting to revive this sense of a common commodity for the Public Good, we searched for inspiration in the architecture and design of the WPA, and the culture that surrounded it.

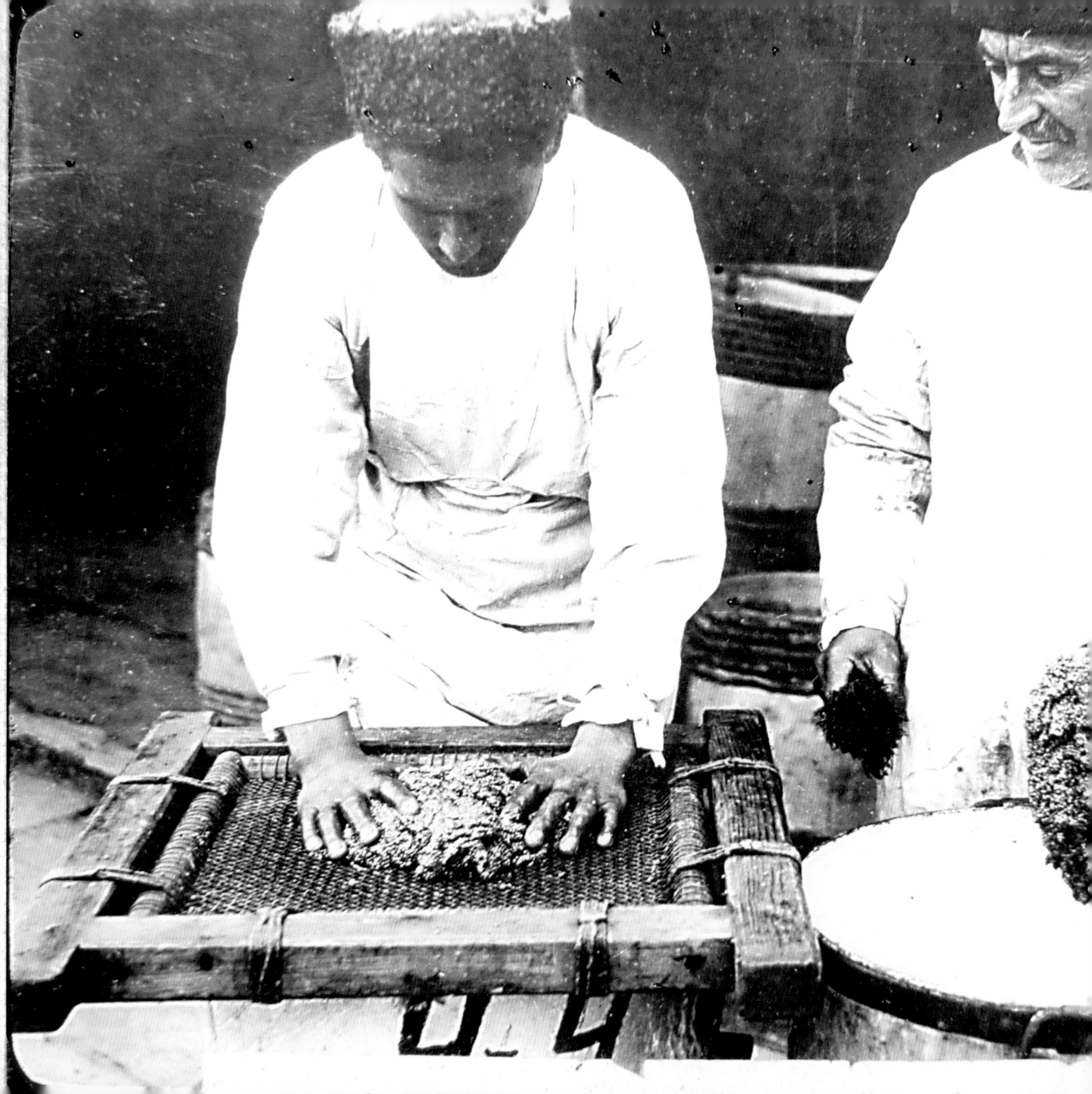

Neg. 1148-56
W.P.A. PROJECT #34

THE EDISON TALE

"Although we typically have a strong sense of what objects we might want to install to support a design concept, sometimes the most relevant items are discovered completely by accident. While we were out and about looking for specific furniture pieces for PUBLIC, one of us literally tripped over a doorstop at the entrance of a store. This particular obstacle turned out to be an upside down cast-iron horse head. It was marked down in price about ten times and basically abandoned, but despite its sad predicament, it still had a certain character which resonated with us, particularly with the Edison story in mind. After a quick negotiation, this casting was transformed from a lowly tool to an exalted monument (in memory of all his poor brethren) and now resides in its iconic spot over the entrance to our back lounge."

When we first acquired 210 Elizabeth Street, we learned of a gruesome tale involving Thomas A. Edison and our current location. In the early 1900s, the legendary inventor evidently had his laboratories on the third floor of the building, and in order to convince New York dignitaries to implement DC power throughout the city, he devised an experiment. Down the street, the neighborhood horses were kept in a stable at Elizabeth and Spring Streets. When the horses became too elderly to work, Edison's men would purchase them and bring them to the laboratory. In front of the invited, politically minded guests, Edison would send a DC electrical current through the horse's body. As DC current isn't overly powerful, the horse would survive. Edison would then send an AC electrical current through the horse, killing it instantly and thus impressing upon these governmental decision makers how much safer the Edison-patented DC power was for the fine citizens of New York.

As homage to what we hope is a myth, we installed a cast-iron horse head mounted on the wall presiding over the bar. The intriguing aspect of Edison having occupied this building, however, is not his alleged mistreatment of animals, but that he was among the first inventors to take into account the idea of mass production while formulating his inventions. The very concept of mass production is one of the key ideas we had hoped to convey through PUBLIC, as it stood for a sense of egalitarianism and accessibility.

COURTHOUSE APPEAL

Born from the English judicial system and therefore steeped in its tradition, the powerful image of the dark wood paneled courthouse is almost identically held in our collective conscience, whether via physical experience or through the power of television and the motion picture industry. Although colonial American courthouses were often built of pine and darkly stained to simulate their cross-Atlantic cousins, builders of courthouses during the WPA era returned to the use of American walnut for paneling, owing much to the government subsidized forestry established throughout the country and the subsequent availability of the material. We utilized walnut (romantically, we hoped, from the same planting initiatives) when designing the back wall of PUBLIC as a modern interpretation of the paneling so prevalent in our municipal system of law and order.

FILAMENT REVIVAL

Although the majority of people today wrongly credit Thomas Edison with having invented the incandescent light bulb (it wasn't even among his 1,093 patents), very little is discussed regarding the over 3000 filaments he was credited with testing in deriving the first widely used Practical Light Bulb. We're not exactly sure which version we employ (although we suspect it to be number 2,637), but for us, a bare exposed filament bulb set within an equally utilitarian white porcelain socket would suffice as a simple nod to Edison's obsessive search.

GALVANIZING FUNCTION

At times, the beauty of a design is not how far one can push its boundaries, but how the design is the result of boundaries, as it is usually more challenging (and oftentimes more satisfying) to test the limits of pragmatics. The steel doors that separate the dining room from the lounge area of PUBLIC are a prime example of this exercise, a solution that combines both form and function born out of necessity.

Having made openings in the party wall to combine two adjoining buildings into one space, we were now required by the NYC Building Code to add a three-hour fire separation at the threshold of these openings. However, the most commonly used institutional fire door wasn't going to figure into the overall vision for the space. Having a company in Massachusetts build custom-designed, galvanized steel doors with the same burning-lead-shield-rope-counterweighted-gravity-assist-sliding-mechanism as turn of the twentieth century models turned out to be a more fitting (and surprisingly more economical) solution. Not only do these doors meet the fire code requirements, but they are handsome in performing this utilitarian task.

UNDERWRITERS LABORATORIES INC.® 19-5-3
CLASSIFIED
SLIDING TYPE FIRE DOOR NO.
FIRE RATING   HR.
TEMP. RISE 30 MIN   F. MAXIMUM

FOLLANSBEE STEEL CORP.
Follansbee Forge
FIRE DOOR STANDARD
IC 20 LBS

"In searching for the three-hour doors, we looked at different salvage places in and out of New York City thinking that someone must be keeping them around. They were always in the ten thousand dollar range though, and we were on a tight budget. We finally found a company in Massachusetts that actually still made them. We called up a man named Bud and described what we were looking for. Bud said, 'Oh, you want one o' them ugly doors? Huh? You New Yorkers are always askin' for them ugly doors!' But, yep, that's what we wanted and Bud had them delivered in two weeks."

THE COLLECTIVE MEMORY

It might strike some as perplexing, but we thought it would be entertaining to give patrons the chance to catch up on some leisure reading while they wait for their table. What better time to read up about the proper protocol for "cutting in" at a debutante dance, or the ideal way to stock a community bomb shelter?

Beyond the obvious amusement, the library is an integral component of PUBLIC's design mission, an opportunity to collect and make accessible publications from the '30s and '40s that best exemplify the idealism and spirit of that era (as well as some of our own quirky interests). From do-it-yourself books to girl scout field guides to cookbooks specializing in Brussels sprout recipes, the PUBLIC library truly covers a broad spectrum and strives to hold publications that are an interesting read for those with eclectic tastes.

Even more than a reading collection, these shelves have evolved to become an information sharing experience. Not only have people contributed books and magazines to the collection, but we have also given away more than a few publications.

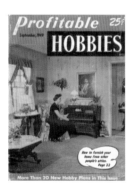 

"Recently, we met a patron who was fanatically interested in trains, and so we took it upon ourselves to send him home with several of our most prized Trains magazines from the PUBLIC library. We hope to never see the magazines again, because exchanges like these make the library more than a design element—it becomes a forum for sharing information that has become tragically obsolete. In the near future, someone will probably bring us ten new magazines on how to crochet tea cozies. We just hope we'll be able to hang on to those for awhile."

47

Public Service

Fifty-Two Sunday Dinners

500 MORE THINGS TO MAKE

COOK

TWENTY LESSONS IN DOMESTIC SCIE

SEXUAL PATHOLOGY

HIRSCHFELD

EMERSON

HUGO'S GERMAN SIMPLIFIED

The PUBLIC SPEAKER'S TREASURE CHEST

PROCHNOW

HARPER

STORIES AND TOASTS

Fowler

A.L.BURT COMPANY

The NEW AMERICAN HOME FIX-IT BOOK

Edited By DOROTHY SARA

BOOKS Inc

C   PUBLIC   PUBLIC   PUBLIC   PUBL   PUBLIC   PUBLIC   PUBLIC   PUBLIC   PUBLIC

A vintage card catalog, which had originally inhabited a New York City public school and was salvaged from a Brooklyn thrift store, lends a familiar warmth to the dining room. In lieu of traditional Dewey Decimal cards, this cabinet stores and catalogs all of PUBLIC's past dinner menus since the day the restaurant opened (each menu iteration is numerically stamped when created, starting with number 0001 on November 3, 2003).

304

Doors to the PUBLIC restrooms were adopted from a pre-war office building. At that time, traditionally painted pressed steel doors were mass-produced to mimic their wood-paneled predecessors. These particular doors still contain the markings of their years of use, including room numbers, notations prohibiting solicitation, and, in an ironic twist, a plaque barring menus.

NO MENUS

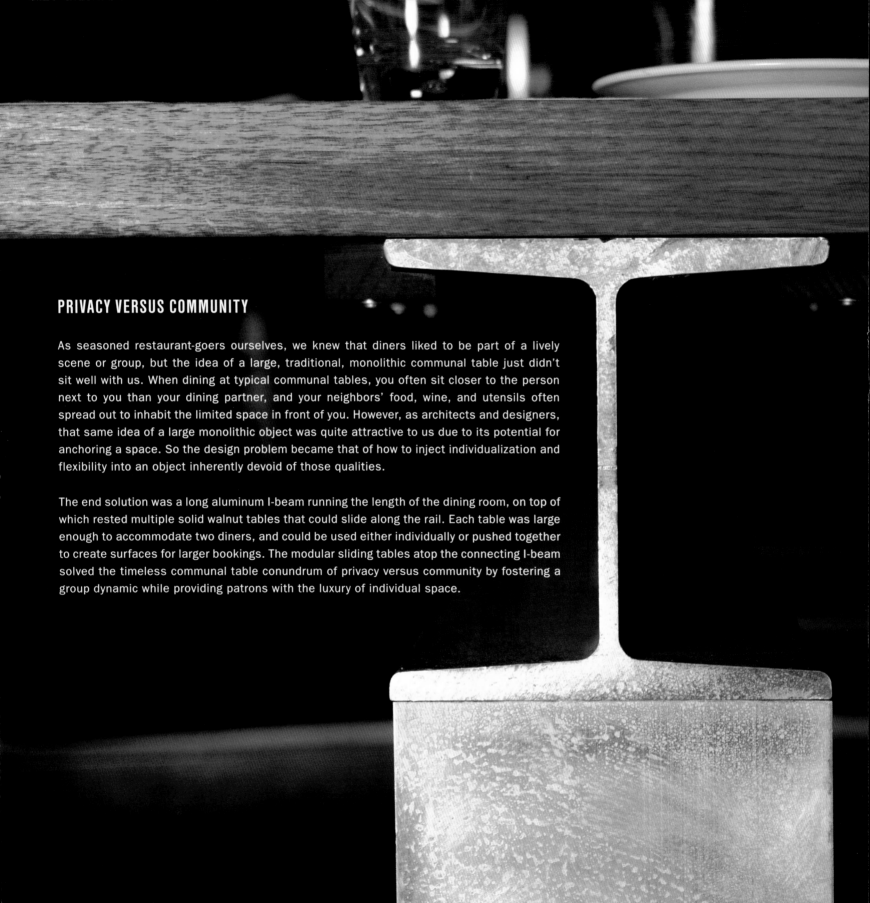

PRIVACY VERSUS COMMUNITY

As seasoned restaurant-goers ourselves, we knew that diners liked to be part of a lively scene or group, but the idea of a large, traditional, monolithic communal table just didn't sit well with us. When dining at typical communal tables, you often sit closer to the person next to you than your dining partner, and your neighbors' food, wine, and utensils often spread out to inhabit the limited space in front of you. However, as architects and designers, that same idea of a large monolithic object was quite attractive to us due to its potential for anchoring a space. So the design problem became that of how to inject individualization and flexibility into an object inherently devoid of those qualities.

The end solution was a long aluminum I-beam running the length of the dining room, on top of which rested multiple solid walnut tables that could slide along the rail. Each table was large enough to accommodate two diners, and could be used either individually or pushed together to create surfaces for larger bookings. The modular sliding tables atop the connecting I-beam solved the timeless communal table conundrum of privacy versus community by fostering a group dynamic while providing patrons with the luxury of individual space.

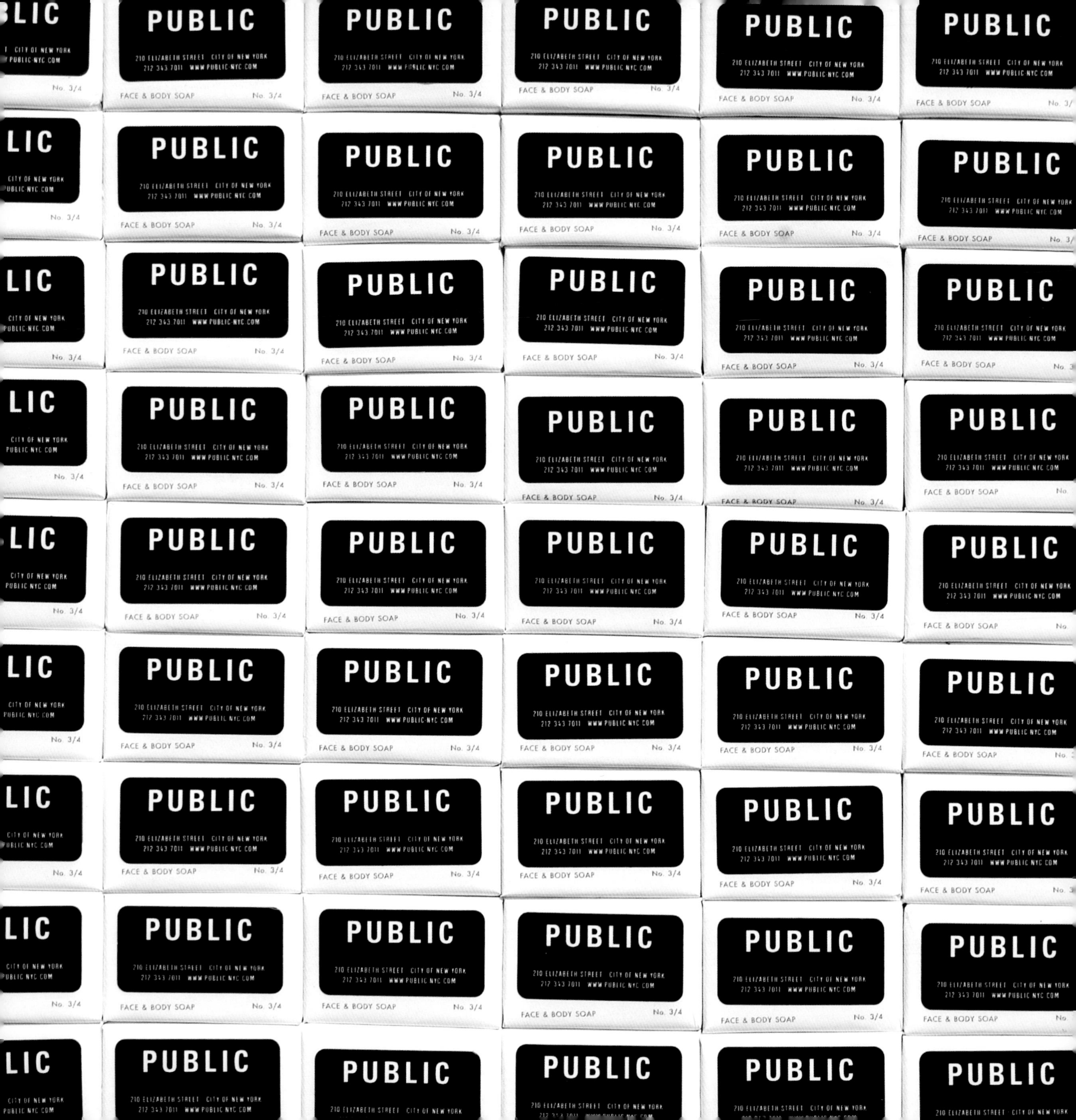
PUBLIC
210 ELIZABETH STREET CITY OF NEW YORK
212 343 7011 WWW.PUBLIC-NYC.COM
FACE & BODY SOAP
No. 3/4

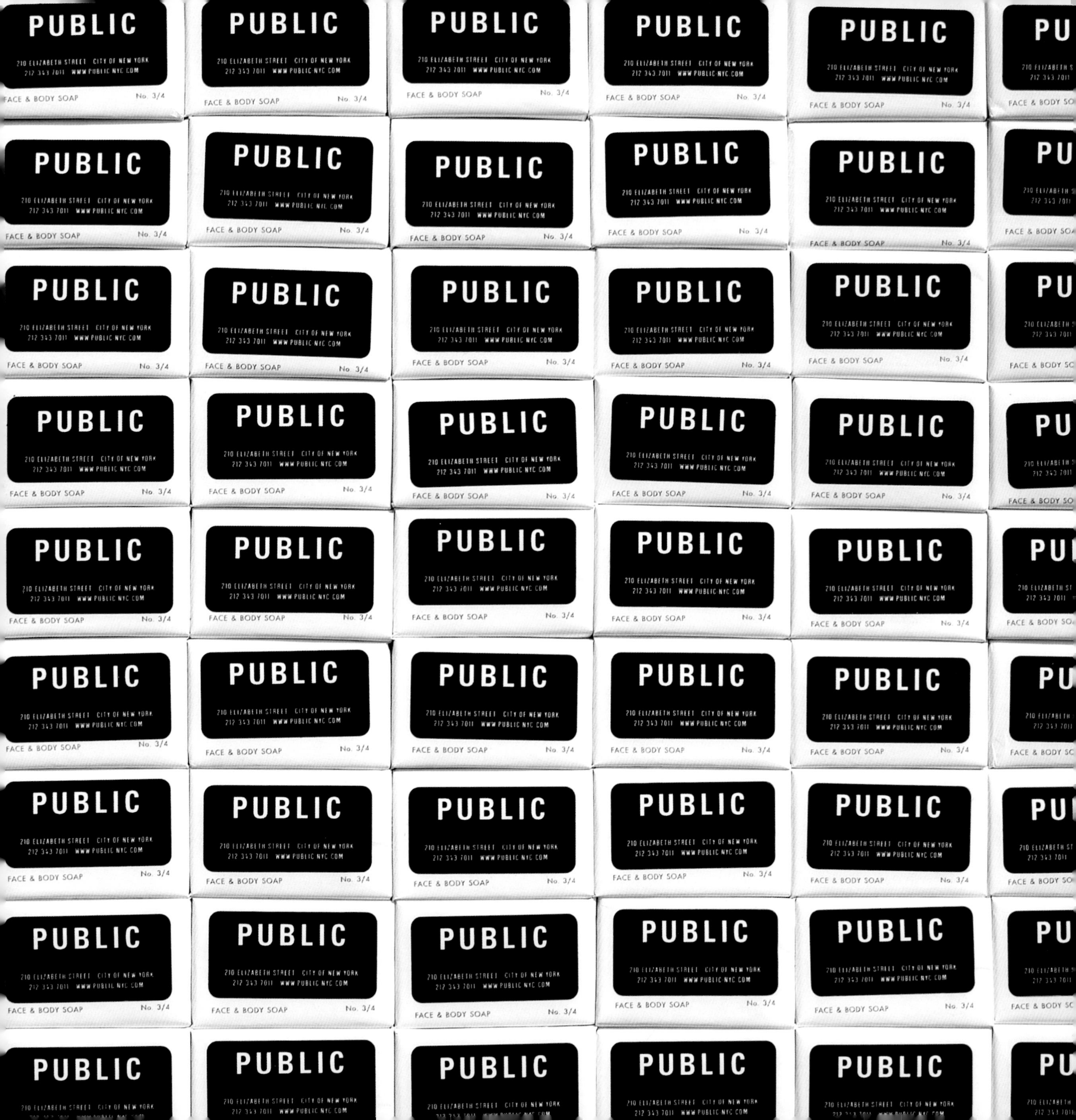
PUBLIC
210 ELIZABETH STREET CITY OF NEW YORK
212 343 7011 WWW.PUBLIC NYC COM
FACE & BODY SOAP
No. 3/4

PUBLIC OFFERING

In late 2003, New York City imposed the infamous smoking ban in all public spaces, including restaurants and bars. Suddenly, the ubiquitous restaurant-branded matchbook seemed much less relevant. We wanted to create a takeaway that was more surprising in form, function, and location—an amusing offering that would catch patrons off guard while remaining memorable and desirable. Asking ourselves what one of the more intriguing locations in the restaurant to find a takeaway might be, the restrooms quickly made the top of the list. As an ode to the spirit of service and grooming that most mid-century washrooms provided, the proliferation of a ridiculous amount of personal soaps became our vehicle. We found the most basic, utilitarian, plain-Jane soaps we could purchase, and co-opted them with a very simple, branded sticker. They immediately resonated with patrons and began disappearing nightly by the purse-load.

CREATING COMMUNITY

The repeating details and rich warmth of PUBLIC's brass post office boxes create an intricate backdrop for an entrance, but ultimately it is this installation's utility that makes its residency in a restaurant setting more appealing. Beyond conceptually following suit with PUBLIC's municipal concerns, these vessels were introduced in order to house a storage and delivery system for our Wine Mailbox Program, creating a dialogue with our own PUBLIC community of like-minded individuals who love adventurous food and unique wine.

For a reasonable fee, patrons rent the P.O. boxes on an annual basis. Each month a unique, hard-to-find bottle of wine, chosen by PUBLIC's Chef Brad Farmerie, is delivered to the address along with his tasting notes, food pairing recommendations, and whatever other odd bits and bobs he wants to dispense (packaged homemade lime pickles, unique corkscrews, etc.)

SHARING TASTE

The idea that the chef can write about finding a fantastic wine, or secrets about the wine or winemaker's history, and then share all of this each month with the patrons is pretty unique. The wine notes he creates are personal, but filled with the kind of information that rounds out the whole wine experience, on both a sensual and technical level.

We had hoped PUBLIC would be filled with ways to connect people emotionally and intellectually; the wine boxes have certainly become a vehicle for that vision.

"Many years ago we made a few (well, more than a few) visits to a local pub in Berlin that seemed to have an incredible warmth and sense of community. The owners had set up a section of lockers where regulars kept their own steins next to a tiny sink for a quick washing. Basically, regulars owned a bit of real estate and were even part of the operations in an odd way. Shared ownership...genius.

"When the time came for us to own our own restaurant, the vision of the pub resurfaced, and we hoped we could create a similar sense of connectivity with regulars through our version of the stein lockers. This was how the Wine Mailbox Program was born, but it has actually grown to be so much more—a vehicle for the chef to share great wine finds, a unique way for people to give wine to friends whom they send along to the restaurant, a connection to great winemakers and even a source of education in wine varietals and their history through monthly wine notes. It's had a tremendous impact for being such a quaint little corner of our operations."

SOLID FOUNDATIONS

Stone plinths and massive concrete cornerstones, due to their natural compressive strength, have been staple architectonic features of banks, libraries, courthouses and other civic structures for centuries, instilling these institutions with a sense of trust and permanence. Poured-in-place, solid concrete structures in PUBLIC attempt to evoke similar emotional reactions by appropriating this material language in modern forms and contexts.

The Roman architect Vitruvius supposedly added animal fat and blood to his concrete mixtures to help them cure quickly, which seemed to work well in structures like the Pont du Gard aqueduct in Nimes, France. Unfortunately for us, the kitchen wasn't operational the morning we poured our concrete plinths, planters, steps, and host stand, so we were sadly unable to follow Vitruvius' recipe.

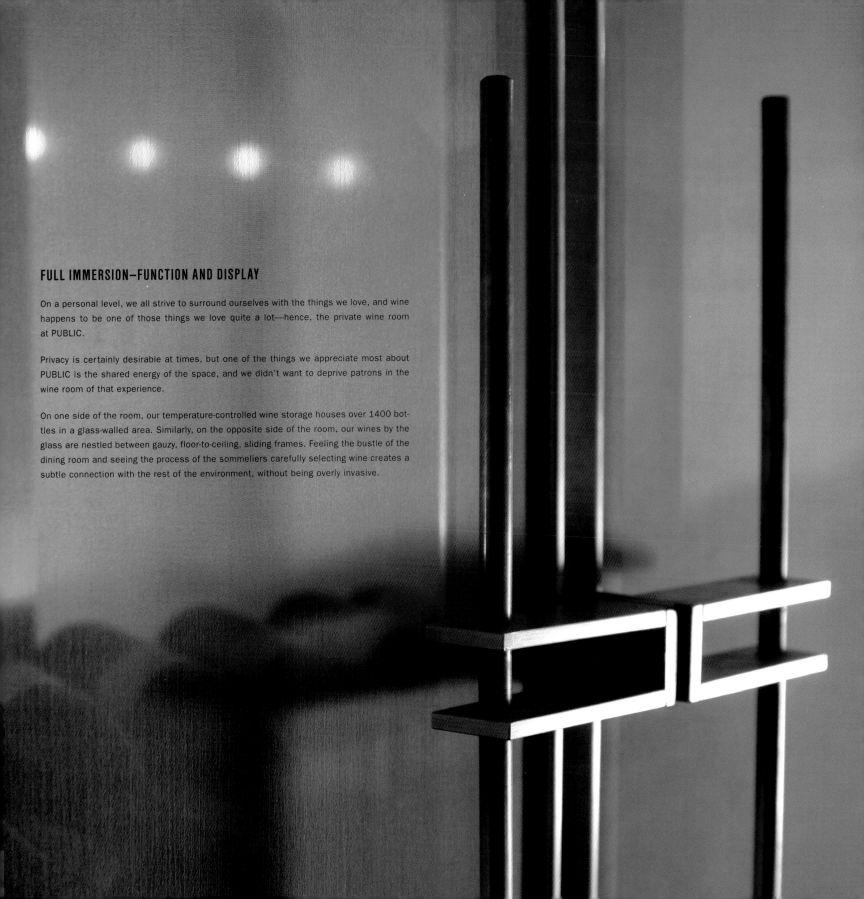

FULL IMMERSION—FUNCTION AND DISPLAY

On a personal level, we all strive to surround ourselves with the things we love, and wine happens to be one of those things we love quite a lot—hence, the private wine room at PUBLIC.

Privacy is certainly desirable at times, but one of the things we appreciate most about PUBLIC is the shared energy of the space, and we didn't want to deprive patrons in the wine room of that experience.

On one side of the room, our temperature-controlled wine storage houses over 1400 bottles in a glass-walled area. Similarly, on the opposite side of the room, our wines by the glass are nestled between gauzy, floor-to-ceiling, sliding frames. Feeling the bustle of the dining room and seeing the process of the sommeliers carefully selecting wine creates a subtle connection with the rest of the environment, without being overly invasive.

City ___BALDWIN_____ State _FLA.__ Phone _____

_____1000__programs_for_Nov._4,_5_____12,_18,_19,_25,_26____

_____ **Frame** _____

Job plate remarks _____ **Ink** _BL__

Art work _____ Type proofs _____

Negative ____2_____ Plate _____2___

Quantity ____1000___ _O_____side_____ **Both sides** ___x_

Finished size _____ Stock name _____Whippet # 16

Press size ____8_____ ___ock color ____White____Can__

_____ _____ _____

Package _____ ___g_____

Stitching _____

Padding _____ Holes or slots _____

Delivered to _Bank_____ Completed __10-20_____
Promised _____
Billed _____OCT 21 1960_____ Amount _____7__

_____ 8 x lines @ 1 0

COST SCHEDULE

PUBLIC

PUBLIC
PRODUCT RECORD

NO. 0008
RM. DINING

$ USD
ITEM

STARTERS

Chilled cassava vichyssoise, Asian pear &
mustard oil salsa, and cassava crisps   8.00

Salad of herby lentils, green beans, avocado,   9.50
toasted pecans & baby gem with pomegranate   19.00
molasses & avocado oil vinaigrette

Abalone mushroom ceviche with miso aubergines   9.00
and a ginger ponzu sauce

Grilled scallops with sweet chili sauce,   14.50
creme fraiche, and green plantain crisps

Squid & seafood ceviche with young coconut,   12.00
Thai herbs, crispy shallots, and a spicy
clear coconut water

Salmon nori roll, pickled lotus root,   11.00
wasabi tobiko, and white soy dipping sauce

Grilled frog legs with three soups   13.00

Pan-seared foie gras, hazelnut brioche, mache   17.00
& edamame salad, and spicy poached pear

Grilled ox tongue, chorizo mash, snake bean   10.00
salad, and tomatillo chutney

Grilled kangaroo on a coriander falafel with   12.00
tahini-lemon sauce and green pepper relish

MAINS

Crispy butternut squash & pinenut stuffed   18.00
brick pastry with pan-fried manouri cheese,
braised cavalo nero, and yuzu dressing

Pan-fried New Zealand snapper on a truffle,   25.00
vanilla & celeriac puree with green beans
and caper salsa

Tasmanian sea trout on a salad of fennel,   21.00
green apple, pistachio and dried gooseberries
with preserved lemon yogurt and fennel pollen

Roast monkfish cheek, saffron potatoes,   22.00
minted courgette & feta salad, and harissa
sauce

Grilled Mayan prawns on wok-fried black beans   24.00
& asparagus, with lump crab and tomato
chili jam

Grilled guinea fowl breast on Indian spiced   22.00
cauliflower and potatoes with apple-black
pepper chutney

Roast lamb chump with quinoa rosti, lemon   23.00
braised fennel, and anchovy mayonnaise

Roast New Zealand venison loin, ginger   25.00
glazed carrots, rainbow chard, and a fig
walnut chutney

SIDES

Green leaf salad   6.00

Sweet potato & miso mash   6.00

Steamed edamame   6.00

Watermelon, feta, and pumpkin seed salad   8.00
with basil

note: gratuity of 20% will be added for tables of 8 or more

CAT. NO. 1-0001 PRINTED IN U.S.A.

PUBLIC

NO. 92201

KRISTINA O'NEAL

PUBLIC
210 ELIZABETH STREET NEW YORK CITY 10012
T: 212.343.7011 F: 212.343.0918
E: kristina@public-nyc.com   www.public-nyc.com

PUBLIC
210 ELIZABETH STREET NEW YORK CITY, NY 10012

F: 212.343.0918   WWW.PUBLIC-NYC.COM

PUBLIC
210 ELIZABETH STREET   CITY OF NEW YORK
212.343.7011   WWW.PUBLIC-NYC.COM
FACE & BODY SOAP   No. 3/4

PUBLIC
210 ELIZABETH STREET   CITY OF NEW YORK
212.343.7011   WWW.PUBLIC-NYC.COM
FACE & BODY SOAP   No. 3/4

Menus are delivered on custom-made, particle board clip-
boards with hand-burnished brass clips. Standard issue
rubber bands secure the bottom of the menu in place.
We have yet to see a rubber band fly across the dining
room during service, but we're sure it's happened.

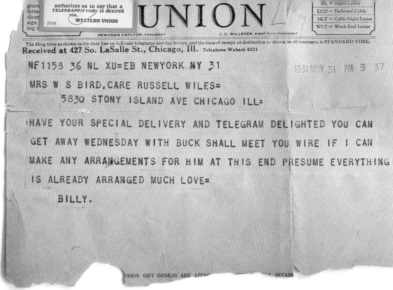

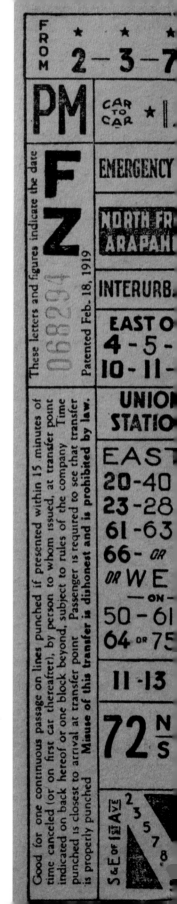

UTILITARIAN STYLE

Inspired by municipal systems and bureaucratic red tape, PUBLIC's graphics sought to capture the essence and beauty of utilitarian style. An extensive search was conducted by the entire office to scavenge aesthetically interesting and relevant printed ephemera in order to identify common themes and practices of the era that we were referencing. Our aim was not to replicate any one particular reference, but rather distill a shared language and modify it to fit our purposes.

STAMPING, RIPPING, NUMBERING AND SIGNING

Of all the examples sourced, certain elements immediately began to stand out and become the basis for the graphic language we would develop. The systems employed for validating, dating, and ordering had inherent psychological overtones of structure, signifying a common faith in authority and desire for authenticity. These methods and their associated tools (stamps, seals, dies, etc.) also created an unintentional yet beautiful narrative on the imperfections of the hand—uneven spacing, the visceral bleed of too much ink, and crooked placement all add great character.

In keeping with this language, we created our own stamps and custom seals. Each menu is hand-stamped, denoting menu version and room. The letterhead and business cards are hand-embossed with a custom PUBLIC seal, and envelopes are hand-stamped with the date before they go out.

DESIGN PRINCIPLE

#02

DECONSTRUCT/ RECONSTRUCT

Most spaces demand that some attention be paid to their history in the re-design, even when there appears to be no physical relationship between the old and new entities. This holds particularly true in Manhattan, where we have run into everything from factories to wineries to churches that were the former inhabitants of the soon to be new restaurant spaces. We will often pull a space apart, both physically and conceptually, then reintegrate historic vestiges into the new design, giving it context and enriched meaning. This type of deconstruction and reconstruction process keeps the spirit of a space intact, and ideally, keeps the resulting design honest as well.

FASHION DECONSTRUCTED

ANDREA STRONG

An ode to the clothiers of the Lower East Side, The Stanton Social is that rare sort of restaurant that inspires gallery-like visits with little need for the fanfare of a meal. People come to The Stanton Social to do more than just eat; they come here to lose themselves in a world where fashion flourished, where seamstresses and haberdasheries occupied every storefront, where the craft of clothing construction was held in the hands of skilled individuals. They come for that unique AvroKO experience.

Like every project that AvroKO tackles, the process of creating, building, and designing The Stanton Social was a multi-layered collaborative experience that began in their airy office loft above a former muffin factory on Elizabeth Street. It was here that I first met with Kristina, Adam, Greg, and William to learn about their integrated design process for a story I was working on for *New York Magazine*. As I witnessed first hand, their work on The Stanton Social was a wildly creative escapade. The journey began with basic questions about the restaurant's neighborhood: What did Stanton Street look like after the turn of the century? What was going on down there?

Like costumers for a period piece, the team began to collect images that would reach back and draw upon the history of the neighborhood, evoking the spirit of that time. "We tried to riff off the location, which at one time was dedicated to the technical art of clothing construction," explained Harris. "We were looking for details from women's clothing and men's suits to inform the design."

They scoured thrift stores, fashion textbooks, and flea markets for objects and images of spaces, textiles, fashion, furniture, clothing—any element that would speak to the specific feeling they were trying to create.

After all the images and elements were collected, they were assembled on large placards called "mood boards"—visual placemats that would become the launch pad for architectural plans, computer images, and sketches that would eventually come to life in brick and mortar. "The mood boards are the heart and soul of the project," O'Neal told me.

Bringing the handiwork of seamstresses and haberdasheries of the Lower East Side into the literal fabric of the design for The Stanton Social—a duplex space—AvroKO decided to devote the ground floor to men's wear and the second floor to women's wear.

To bring this duality to life, the ground floor, which houses the main dining room, a front lounge, and a small oyster bar, was detailed with masculine accents. The walls were earth toned, the banquettes covered in herringbone fabric, and the pillows accented with leather belts from one of the still-standing leather purveyors around the corner. The herringbone motif was traced through to the wine storage wall on the mezzanine, which was created in a herringbone pattern, with each angular slot refrigerated and built to hold a case of wine. To build a sense of community, the team designed the dining room with semi-circular banquettes so that diners faced each other and the center of the room. Inspired by the construction of a man's classic shoe, with its sturdy leather sole and soft leather upper, AvroKO used two different leathers for the banquettes.

The upstairs, which houses a bar, lounge, and a small dining area, was the feminine yin to the masculine yang. The warmer space was designed to be flirtatious, with alluring, sexy, feminine details: hourglass-shaped lampshades that recall the boning of old-fashioned undergarments, walls covered in soft fringe, a bar designed like the links of a delicate wristwatch, silk floral dressing screens, and salvaged vintage hand mirrors collected from flea markets and antique shops. The effect is a lounge hushed with a feminine mystique.

Like the physical design of the space, the collateral materials—menus, business cards, matches, and the like—also nod to this former garment center neighborhood. Each of these materials bear the restaurant logo, which is The Stanton Social signature written in a script similar to a hand-signed designer label from a suit jacket. Even the waiter's uniforms are tagged with sewn-on "The Stanton Social" signature labels.

The cumulative effect of these details is a space that is arrestingly tactile, vibrating with the life of another era, and yet avoiding any outright nostalgia. This overall duality of The Stanton Social sets your mood, manipulates your reality, and leaves you with a sensation that remains with you long after you have finished your meal and strolled back into the night on Stanton Street.

FINDING IT

The initial process of analyzing an existing space can yield a number of preliminary design ideas and directions. Sometimes these ideas are born from a space's materiality, but oftentimes the design potential stems from the nature of the existing architecture. At The Stanton Social, the stunning 16-foot-high tin ceilings on the ground floor would only serve as an amuse bouche to the real opportunities lying literally around it. That this was a two-story space granted us the flexibility to pursue ideas that can't be achieved in a typical (for Manhattan) single-story space. A glowing, herringbone patterned wine wall is interesting, but it becomes that much more potent when asked to span two stories, tying the restaurant together both programmatically and conceptually.

MENDING IT

"If it's not broken, don't fix it." However, from time to time it might be okay to throw a rock through the window to precipitate a bit of mending. The conditions of the existing façade, despite containing some gorgeous steelwork, were rough at best. Despite a desire to throw a big rock and start from absolute scratch, we confined our focus to reconfiguring the entry doors to create a slight vestibule and refinished the steel to its natural beauty.

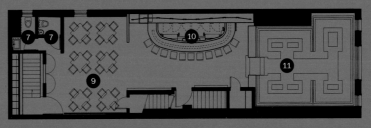

SECOND FLOOR

1. ENTRY

2. HOST

3. WAITING LOUNGE

4. OYSTER BAR

5. GROUND FLOOR DINING

6. SERVICE BAR

7. RESTROOM

8. MEZZANINE DINING

9. SECOND FLOOR DINING

10. BAR

11. LOUNGE

12. KITCHEN

13. OFFICE

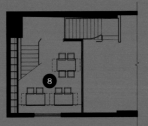

MEZZANINE

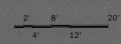

2' 8' 20'
4' 12'

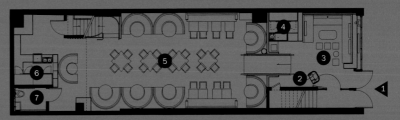

GROUND FLOOR

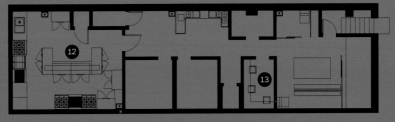

BASEMENT

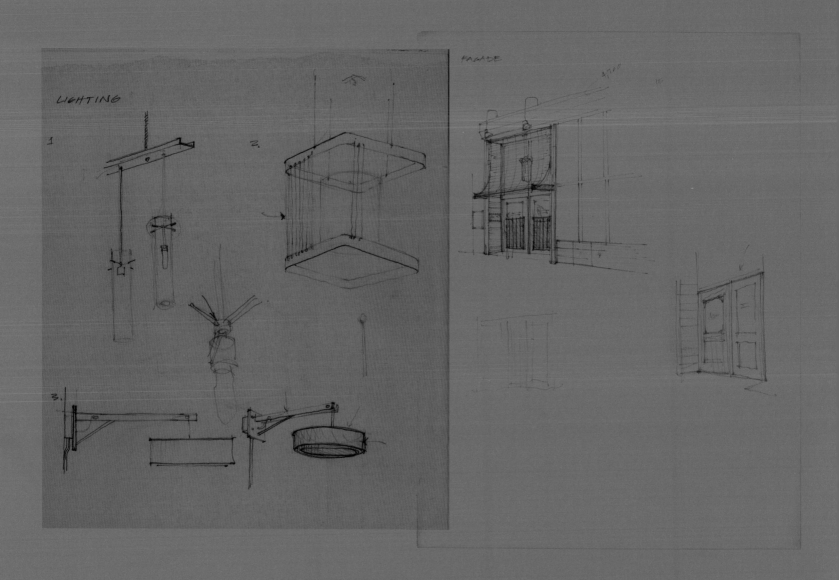

LIGHTING

FAÇADE

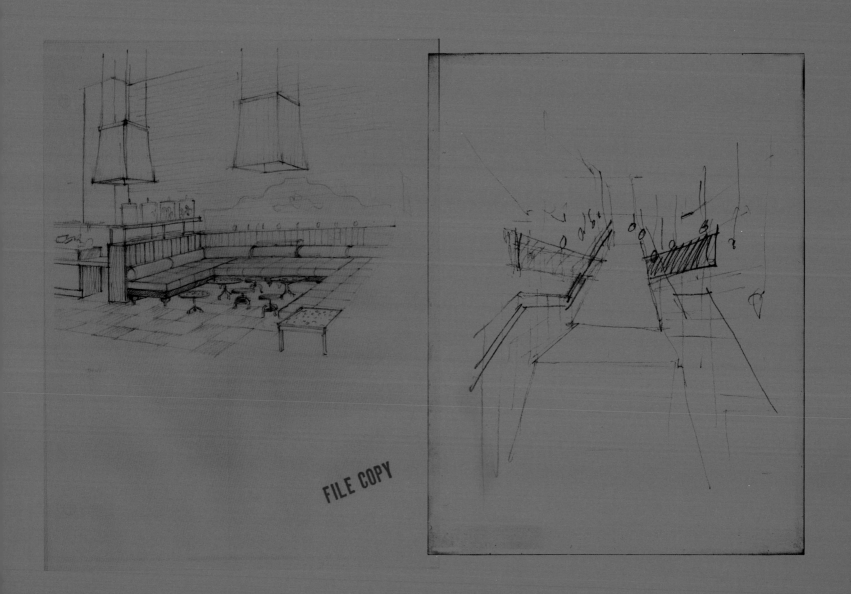

SEARCH & DESTROY

Over forty vintage men's suits were purchased from three different states as part of the discovery process for The Stanton Social fashion references. Each piece was deconstructed to find the interesting shapes and forms that could be used as inspiration and applied as details in the architecture, furniture, and art installations. We were fascinated by the complexity of the suits' construction, concealed between the typically rich material that served as the garment's exterior and its silky lining. In a way, this was the perfect analogy to our practice of taking apart a physical space to expose its history and original construction, asking the structure of the existing architecture to inform the environment we aim to construct.

"We scoured every junk shop, thrift store, and vintage boutique in the tri-state area looking for interesting suits that might have some hidden facet we could use as inspiration for the space. It's important to note, though, that we often spend copious amounts of time searching for and buying things that don't actually get used in the project. This was certainly the case for these poor suits, in the literal sense, but they did become the spark for many of the more unexpected design ideas. We aren't restrained when it comes to the physical discovery process as it often becomes our strongest lifeline to fluid thinking... right up to the day before opening."

DOMINATING PATTERNS

The tin ceiling is original to the space, circa 1923, so of course it had to be preserved. The quiet, square pattern of the tin provided a foil and a sense of regularity to the more activated fashion-based patterns that were added as spatial elements. The pewter paint was the final touch for modernization.

MAN ABOUT TOWN

The classic herringbone pattern is an extremely strong visual cue, especially when blown out of its typical scale. Appropriating its configuration, the slanting forms of the herringbone made a surprisingly adept structure for a wine wall. Capitalizing on the lofty ceilings, this massive two-story structure became not only a powerful aesthetic statement on the main floor, but also a functional element that unified the downstairs dining room with the upstairs lounge. The lights and darks of the herringbone pattern were created using dark-stained oak shelving in contrast to the warm, incandescent glow of the cabinet's backlight.

A GENTLEMAN'S DETAILS

While conceptualizing the ground floor space at The Stanton Social, we took some time to discuss how to represent men's fashion in less obvious ways. This meant not only drawing details from the physical deconstructed material elements in men's fashion, but also extrapolating from the masculine patterns and color combinations found in men's conservative formal wear.

"For the longest time in the design process, we had a clean grid of steel cables that riffed off of the grid of the ceiling to create each individual wine receptacle. This was proving to be an expensive endeavor. Then one of our clients looked down at the herringbone fabric that we'd been showing him for over two months and said (we wonder now if he was half joking), 'how 'bout a herring bone wine wall?' We immediately said 'absolutely' and began calculating how big each herring had to be to fit a case of wine."

ON BEING SOCIAL

Design that is simply visually pleasing tends to be flat and one-dimensional; after all, the beauty in most things is how they are experienced. Ultimately, design can be a vehicle for inducing a certain sensation or eliciting a desired emotional response.

To that end, The Stanton Social was to be more than just a pretty face for a restaurant. As its name implied, the restaurant was about encouraging a collective social experience, achieved through both the layout of the space and the small plates menu that promoted sharing. The rounded banquettes (coveted by our client) flanking both sides of the space were designed to face into the center of the dining room for two purposes: to promote interaction at the table, as well as to encourage an interface across the space as a whole. There is an energy shared by everyone in the restaurant which begins with the patrons on the main floor, is lifted to the diners on the mezzanine, and then is discreetly whispered to the guests in the lounge upstairs.

"While we were researching the time period, one of the things that really struck us was how people went all out when they would go to dinner during the '20s and '30s. It wasn't about how wealthy you were. It didn't matter what economic or social class you were in. You always put on your best when you were out on the town. This is what we hoped to bring into the space, this sense of up-scale elegance, a curious juxtaposition in the gritty Lower East Side.

"It's a bit odd how they coexisted in our minds—the construction and deconstruction of fashion and the social element of the upper crust putting fashion on display. It was a simultaneous line of thinking, joining the two worlds together through hints more than anything else."

THE NEW 400

Oftentimes, successful design is achieved through eliciting harmony from contradictions. The above photograph of a classic, swank dinner party from turn-of-the-century New York made a lasting impression on us. The image of the communal banquet table and the shared dining experience, lavish with a touch of whimsy, was almost exactly the mood we wanted to capture at The Stanton Social. However, it was more than a little paradoxical that the experience we sought to create was inspired by the fabled New York "400" lifestyle (the "400" referred to the number of people that would fit in Mrs. William Astor's ballroom, the uppermost echelon of New York society), a way of life that was completely at odds with that of the Lower East Side during the same historical period. The Stanton Social neighborhood of the early 1900s was not one of glamorous balls and summering in Newport, but rather one of immigrant struggles and overcrowded tenements.

As we delved further into our design development, we realized we could bring about a sense of accord to these disparate socio-economic states. We could pay respect to the neighborhood's garment district roots, while utilizing this design direction to create a new, modern space for a more democratic version of this type of swish dinner party.

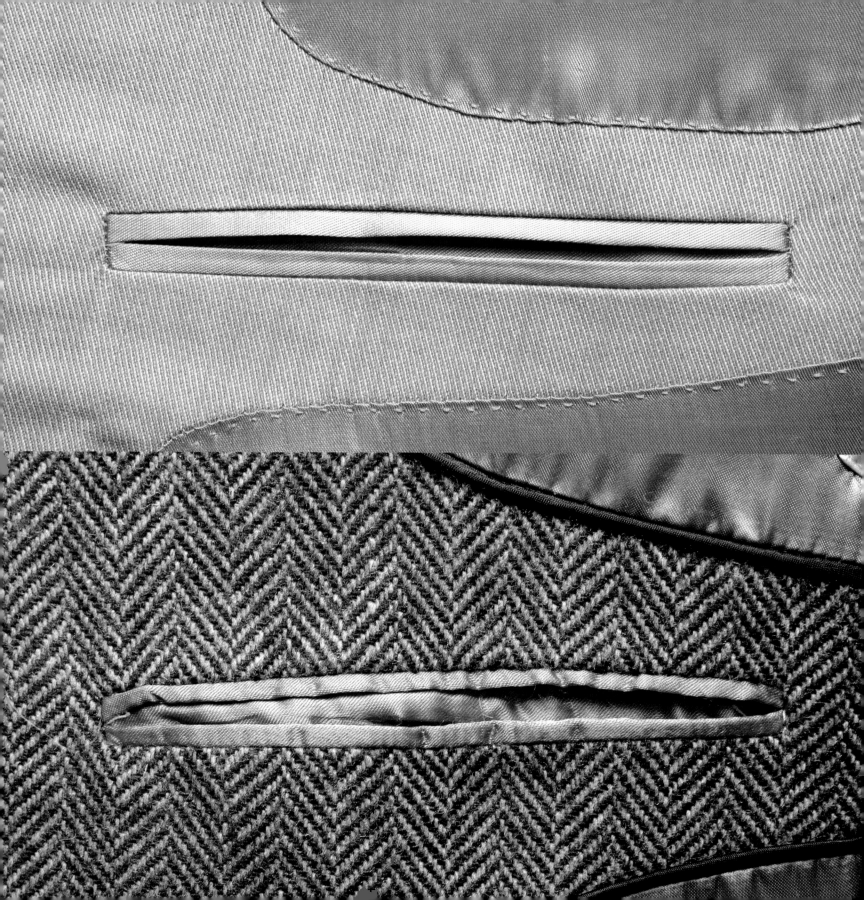

THE LABEL PURSUIT

Part of our obsession with vintage men's suits led to an equally intriguing fascination with the embroidered clothing tags sewn within the jackets—symbols of authenticity and the clothier's pride in craftsmanship. Wanting to include some vestiges of these symbols into the space, several variations of the installation at the entrance were developed before the current one was actually chosen. For the final image, a vintage clothing tag was clipped, photographed, and intensely magnified to remove it from its typical context and create an abstraction of the original. Even the elongated form was based on a coat tag format—long and rectangular.

ADJUSTABLE FIT

In the ground floor waiting area, handcrafted leather belts were used to attach loose pillows that could be moved along a top bar for flexible seating. The issue of creating flexible seating mechanisms sometimes provokes new ideas purely because obvious solutions typically won't work. Creative ideas have to be developed to increase the functionality and efficiency of a space, no matter how many people are seated there. From that point, visually interesting ideas often spring into form with the "engineering" aspect in full consideration.

INTIMATE INSPIRATION

As a counterpoint to the ground floor rooted in masculinity, the second floor of The Stanton Social conceptually acquired the air of a lady's boudoir—everything from sumptuous lizard skin banquettes in deep red hues to fringed panels inspired by flapper dresses of the '20s, to a back bar inspired by the links of a lady's bracelet or watch. However, the focal point of the room is its perimeter: twenty backlit dressing screens inspired by vintage kimono designs. As night falls, these screens exude a sense of mystery among the dim glow of candlelight, creating the notion that another more intimate (and off limits) space might reside just beyond the panels.

CINCHED

The corset-inspired light fixtures were designed specifically to suit the more feminine-oriented upstairs lounge. The light's form is a riff on the hourglass corset without being literal to this garment's strict proportioning guidelines. Using spring steel for the stiffening ribs, the corset's bone-in structure is emphasized when the light shines through the translucent muslin sheathing.

CHEEKY DETAILS AND HAPPY INCIDENTS

The act of sourcing objects for design inspiration, reference, or for use in an installation, is often a serendipitous one. This phenomenon, in which objects present us with a previously unforeseen or unexpected layer of authenticity, character, and honesty, we sometimes call a "Happy Incident." Within the collection of hand mirrors alone were plenty of Happy Incidents: curious bird prints, ornate silver Victorian damask details, classic gold inlays on ivory—all of which were part and parcel to the individual character of the mirrors, rendering each one unique.

SNEAK PEEK

We take great pride and pleasure in introducing function and utility to what are generally considered merely decorative objects whenever possible. In the upstairs lounge, the vintage hand mirror installation's beautiful physical qualities add to the lounge's sense of intimacy and femininity; typically found on a woman's vanity, these mirrors are one of her most personal possessions. Alternatively, the inclusion of these small but exquisite objects in the low-lit lounge scene very subtly encourages the art of flirtation, allowing patrons to quickly and discreetly catch their reflections and make any necessary cosmetic adjustments without missing a social step. In their own delicate way, the mirrors play an integral role in contributing to the elegantly seductive lounge experience.

FUNCTION FOLLOWS FORM

During our research phase, we came across an image of a unique crinoline, circa 1865, and were immediately taken with it. The intricate skeletal steel form, which women in the nineteenth century wore underneath their dresses to support the voluminous shapes of their skirts, symbolized to us the full narrative of fashion, that the beauty of a garment's decorative exterior was made possible through the careful consideration of its interior construction. We extrapolated the essential components of the crinoline—the linen strips and steel wire hoops—to inform the detailing of the design elements within the entry, most notably the stair wall. The sense of the structure is evident, despite substituting leather strips for linen and reworking the pattern to accentuate the height of the space.

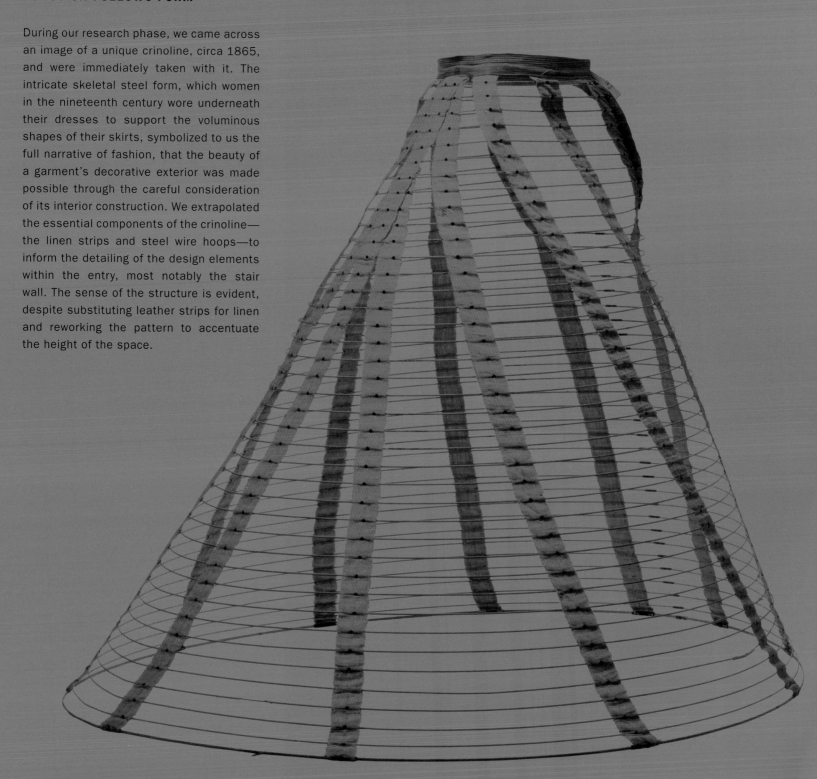

LINE OF SIGHT

The idea of continuity within a space is extremely important, whether through materiality, scale, form, detail, or simple visual access. Preserving a sense of common energy across distinct and separated spaces, especially in a restaurant with such communal goals as The Stanton Social, informed many design decisions. Within the stairwell to the second floor lounge, an otherwise fully separated experience due to its role as an egress corridor, the insertion of a slim window goes great distances to connect people visually to the rest of the restaurant. However, the window's slightly unusual height and placement was designed to force the seeing to be seen, offering patrons in the main dining area a framed voyeuristic glimpse of those in the stair heading to the lounge.

"This staircase became a particularly difficult assignment. Ideally, we would have left an open staircase indicating to people the existence of an upstairs. Because of the two-hour fire wall required by code, enclosing the whole thing in glass would have cost about $50,000. So, we resorted to a fire-rated glass door system to create a connection directly at the hostess stand to the upstairs, and then included this perfectly proportioned slot that allows both sides of the space to view each other. We think this works especially well for those going upstairs as they get a glimpse of the diners on the first floor. It also makes for a compelling composition of glass and leather from the first-floor perspective of the space."

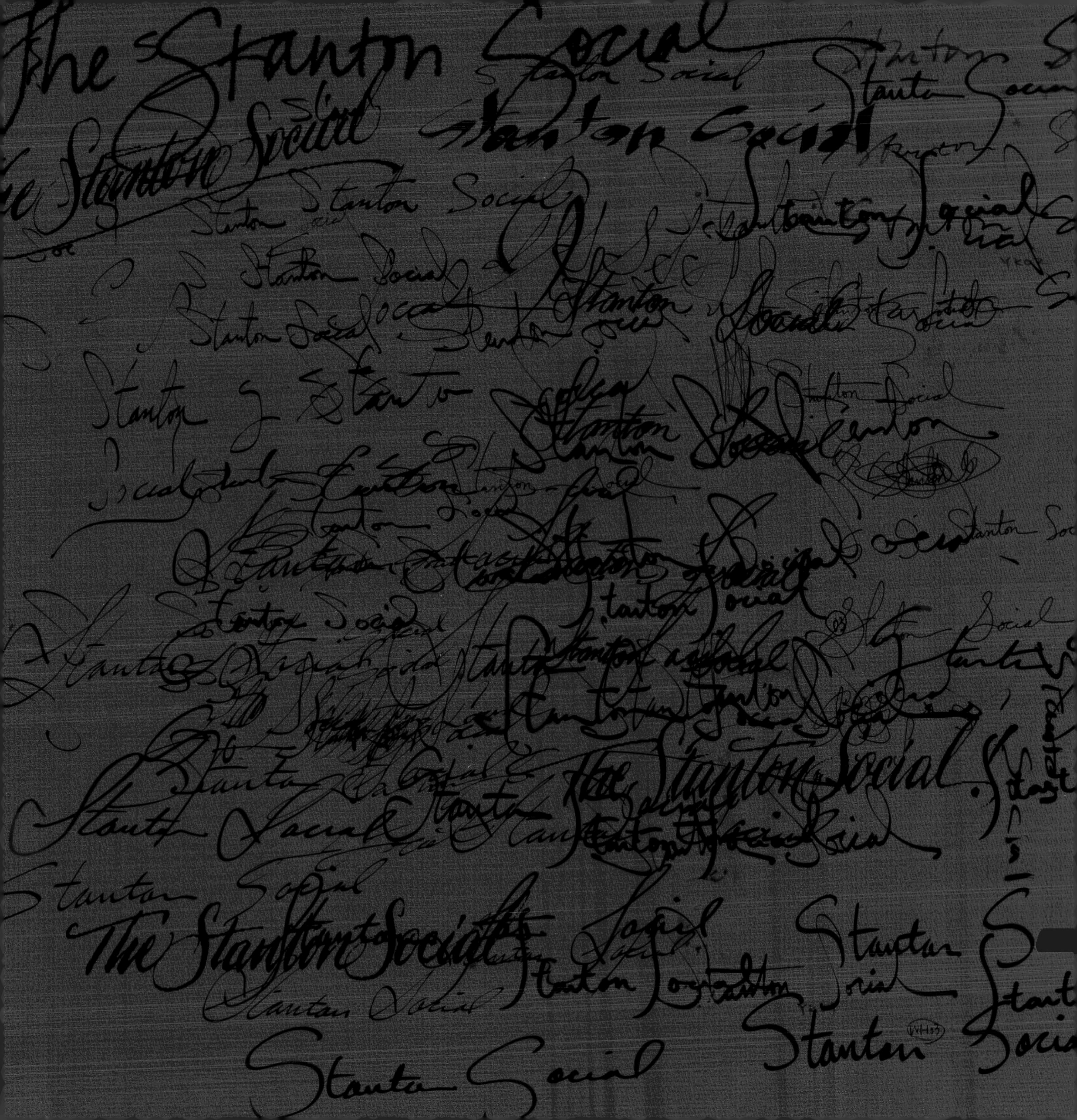
The Stanton Social
Stanton Social
Stanton Social
Stanton Social
The Stanton Social
The Stanton Social
Stanton Social
Stanton Social

A COLLABORATIVE EFFORT

Creating The Stanton Social logo would turn out to be quite a labor intensive affair. Influenced by classic fashion label signatures, and not wanting to ignore these inherent symbols of authenticity, it seemed obvious that we had to create a new font so that the logo would resonate as "original." The first stage of the process involved getting samples from eight different professional script calligraphers, but realizing that their writing was far too stylized (and to some degree, not flawed enough to be personal or natural), we turned to everyone on our staff and asked them to take turns handwriting "The Stanton Social" enough times to cover a full sheet of paper. After more than fifty sheets were completed, the final selection was chosen that best embodied the script for this new, modern label.

the *Stanton Social*

lower east side

DECONSTRUCTION

Finding inspiration is not the difficult part in the design process; figuring out what to do with it, in an original and creative way, is more complicated. Unearthing these incredible shoes from 1926 at a nondescript vintage store, we were immediately struck by their craftsmanship and individuality. Compared to the mass-produced shoes of today, these felt like small, limited-edition works of art. The personal signature stamped on each, the handwritten sizing delicately inscribed on the interior, and the evidence of human touch would begin a path of analyzing other typically mass-produced materials and our potential to make them more personal.

RECONSTRUCTION

Restrooms are naturally great places to experiment with materials, as they are typically small spaces and contained experiences. This, then, would be the perfect place to create a modern interpretation of the vintage shoe markings. Drawing upon the idea of royal crests often seen in vintage clothing and watermarked fabric, we appropriated an old illustration that was then hand-silk-screened onto wall panels and glazed to become massive un-mass-produced tiles. The result is that the restrooms somewhat resembled the interior of a jewelry box, with lush burgundy walls and twinkling Art Deco touches via perfume bottle-like flower vases.

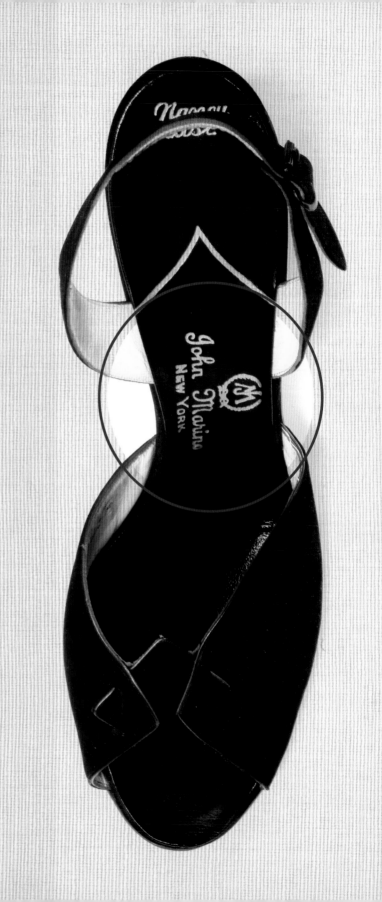

The Principle of Deconstruct/Reconstruct is strangely evident in the restrooms. Classic crest forms were silk-screened in a random pattern, and in many areas where they intersect with corners, or the floor or ceiling, the images consequently become dissected and fragmented, creating a sense that they extend well beyond the confines of the room. The high gloss of the red laminate beneath them is extremely reflective, so where fragmented images die into a corner or mirror they are reconstructed to seem whole again. This illusion really starts to break down the expected visual planes of the room, making them seem almost translucent, and adds a surreal sense of otherworldliness.

KEEPING A TIGHT HOLD

Menu design and production has a lot to do with function—how the menu is held together, how the paper element works with the physical or rigid components, how it can be stacked and carried by servers, how easy it is to read, how menu items are grouped, etc. All of these considerations are then followed by the question, "What can make the menu a unique experience while maintaining consistency with the other elements of the architecture and design?"

For The Stanton Social, the answer was to create a completely custom object melding masculine materials with feminine details to provide a visceral but uncomplicated experience. Solid, custom-cut walnut boards were notched to accommodate elastic straps (literally the very same used in women's undergarments) dyed to match the color of the identity. This construction served the dual purpose of securely holding the menu paper in place while making it convenient for the staff to change out new menu versions. The most satisfying feature, however, is surely the sound the straps make when snapped against the rigid board.

"Of all the menus we've designed, these are certainly the ones most often stolen. It's fairly shocking. Within the first year we had to produce three batches of these, increasing the quantities every time, and still it was never enough. Whether it's just the bands or the whole menus, these have a way of walking out the door. We think it's the tactile materiality and playfulness that captures peoples' imaginations, and then results in them cuddling up under a roomy overcoat."

the *Stanton Social*
lower east side

SWEETS TO SHARE

Flight of Souffle's - chocolate, meyer lemon & raspberry $8

Valrhona Dark Chocolate Fondue
homemade marshmallows, peanut butter rice krispies & wild strawberries $8

Jamie's Cookies & Milk
chocolate chip, social-o's, oatmeal raisin & baby black & whites $7

Ice Cream Sandwiches
peanut butter & jelly, cookies & cream, strawberry shortcake $7

Lavender - honey & vanilla **Creme Brulee** $8

Frozen Lime Semifreddo $7

Warm Doughnuts with caramel $6

Cheese Plate
Creamy Humboldts Fog Cheese with grilled raisin brioche &

AFTER DINNER DRINKS

Espresso $3.25   Cappuccin

Coffee $3   Calvados 12 yr Camut

Chateau de Bria

DESIGN PRINCIPLE

#03

ELEVATING
INDUSTRIAL

We all believe that there is an inherent (but oftentimes overlooked) beauty in industrial forms and materials. The pragmatic purity of hardware, designed solely with function in mind, exudes an unpretentious honesty, while the solidity of steel and concrete conjure an air of reliability and strength. While many industrial elements on their own can be rough and lowly, with the right applications and juxtapositions, they can be elevated to a refined level...possibly even becoming poetic.

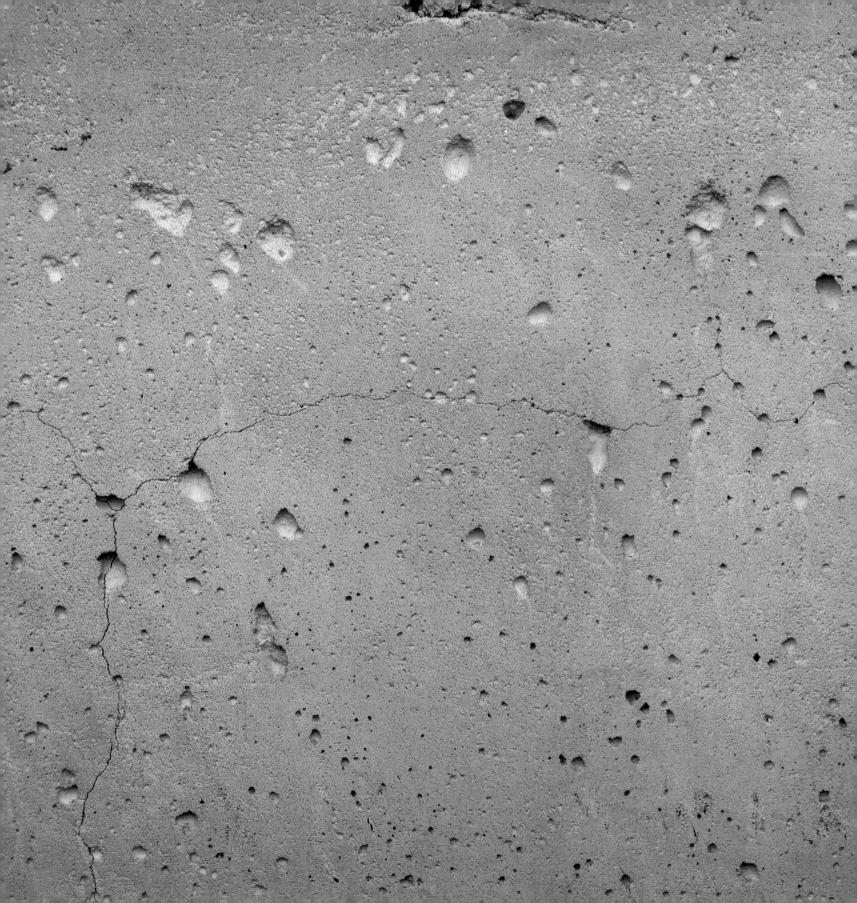

SAPA

THE MAKING OF A HILL STATION

JEN RENZI

A buzzy restaurant/lounge in New York's Flatiron district, Sapa exemplifies AvroKO's highly conceptual approach to its craft, while proving that brainy, clever design need not preclude a strong dose of nuance and sex appeal. Like AvroKO's previous projects, Sapa is at once coolly intellectual and engagingly visceral.

Duality is the name of the game for the interior scheme as well, which mirrors the menu's idiosyncratic take on French-Vietnamese cuisine. Sapa's menu is not a fusion of those two influences; rather, dishes are either French or Vietnamese in origin. Likewise, the interior takes opposing elements and plays them off one another: rough against refined, primitive against modern, gauzy against muscular. Fleshy exposed-concrete surfaces, pockmarked with cracks and fissures, are counter-pointed by super-sleek backlit onyx. Ethereal lanterns that float throughout the space are counterbalanced by the earthbound pull of dark-stained wood banquettes. Organic elements like an enfilade of topiaries play off a rigorous, industrial succession of grids that define wall and ceiling planes. "The architecture is not about merging cultural elements," explains Harris. "It's about the coexistence of unique moments."

AvroKO projects are always imbued with a strong sense of history, and Sapa is no exception. The bifurcated aspect of Sapa's cuisine and design is a hearty nod to its namesake, a Vietnamese French-colonial vacation town. The exotic locale is distinguished by a split-personality architectural vernacular; here,

you'll find a French chateau standing right alongside a traditional Vietnamese villa, and the coexistence of very different craft traditions that never experienced miscegenation. "All along the hillsides, you'll see a perfectly pristine white French house nestled in the odd, rugged Vietnamese backdrop," says O'Neal. "Really opposing elements beside each other that don't quite make sense," adds Bradshaw.

Rough and refined, ornate and streamlined. Sapa is not about "either/or" but about "and." AvroKO's approach is dialectic rather than synthetic: opposites are kept in dynamic balance. The genius of AvroKO's design is how layered and nuanced it is, and how the layering acts as a sort of binding agent between the opposing forces. The designers coax out similarities within differences, exposing the underlying logic of seemingly disparate details. Rough concrete and boldly veined onyx do indeed contrast, but AvroKO treated these surfaces in a conceptually similar fashion so both read as expressions of pure texture. And take the bartop, a barcode-like amalgam of mahogany-stained wood planks of varying widths, and the roll bar, laminated from slim vertical onyx strips. And pay attention to the grid, an element that's repeated in various locations, but in differing materials: concrete beams crisscrossing the ceiling, the iron framework of the staircase, and the glass-and-steel window wall separating eating areas from the kitchen.

At Sapa, AvroKO's holistic approach is evident in the strong synergy between cuisine and interior. The four partners have a practical,

hands-on understanding of how a restaurant works, from space flow to menu stations to the choreography of the kitchen. "I've personally worked as everything from busboy to manager," says Farmerie. "I understand a back waiter's job relative to a server's job relative to the job of getting food out of a kitchen. This level of understanding drives a responsible design, one that supports how people need to move through space."

At Sapa, smart traffic patterns weave throughout a series of intimate zones with different moods. Tantalizing sightlines between them lend a sense of mystery, movement, and excitement. In addition to the main dining space there's a self-contained lounge with low couches near the entrance, the central Vietnamese roll station, the mahogany bar near the open kitchen, and a brick-walled back room raised two steps above the main floor, which can double as a private party space. To preserve the loft-like proportions, the restaurant is divvied up not by solid walls, but by differences in seating height and material treatment, the lantern-like muslin-wrapped staircase, and other elements that are as much psychological devices as physical entities.

AvroKO's genius is not just great design, but psychologically charged spaces that always feel new and surprising and never gimmicky. In an era defined by over-the-top gestures, eating-as-theater, and even idiosyncratic gems knocking themselves off ad nauseum, it's very hard to succeed as AvroKO does, trafficking in subtleties, smarts, and nuance.

REINCARNATION

In its previous life, the Sapa space was a church administration office and bookstore, adorned in an unfortunate combination of lilac and yellow. Drywall enveloped the majority of the interior, and wall-to-wall carpet in a "corporate-friendly" pattern covered the floors. There were, however, some redeeming features behind the current trappings of the century-old building. With a little caution (and a fair bit of demolition), we were able to restore a few architectural elements of the original interior, including the dilapidated but gorgeous steel casement windows on the North wall, and old Greek revival plaster moldings on the numerous columns throughout the space. Bets were on the table that once the ceiling was shed of its drywall and dropped acoustic panels, the board-formed concrete beams and ceiling above would be worth salvaging as well.

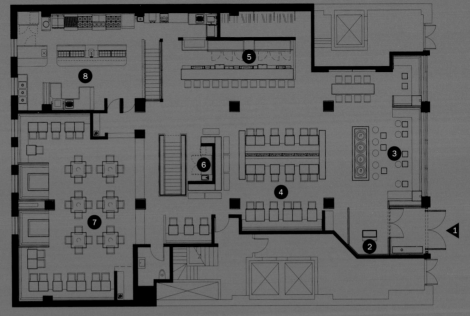

GROUND FLOOR

1. ENTRY

2. HOST

3. LOUNGE

4. FRONT DINING

5. BAR

6. ROLLS BAR

7. BACK DINING

8. KITCHEN

9. RESTROOM LOUNGE

10. RESTROOMS

11. OFFICES

12. KITCHEN PREP

BASEMENT

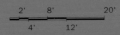

2' 8' 20'
4' 12'

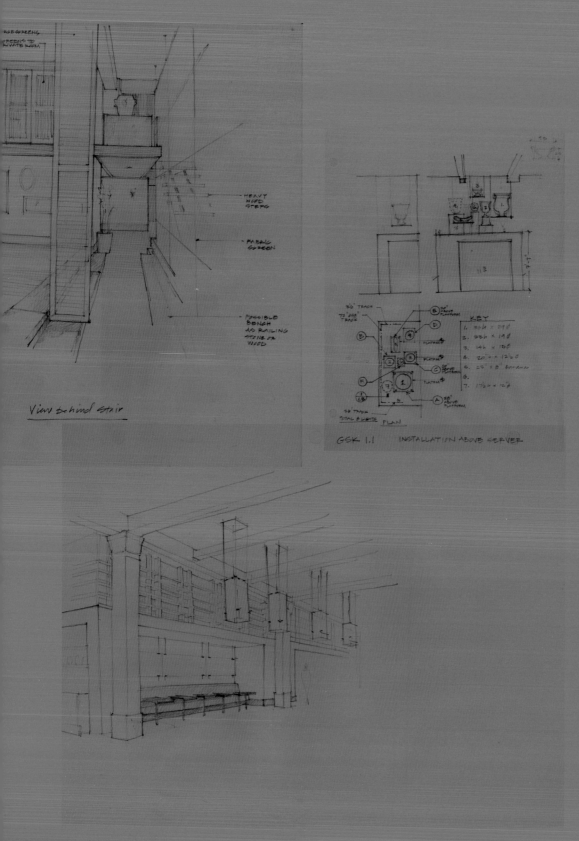

View behind stair

HEAVY
WOOD
STEPS

FABRIC
SCREEN

POSSIBLE
BENCH
AS RAILING
STONE OR
WOOD

KEY
1. 36h × 21∅
2. 53h × 19∅
3. 14h × 15∅
4. 20 × 12∅∅
5. 25' × 8' overall
6.
7. 17½h × 12∅

PLAN

GSK 1.1   INSTALLATION ABOVE SERVER

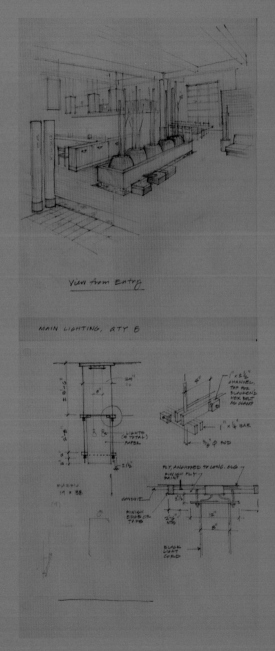

View from Entry

MAIN LIGHTING, QTY 8

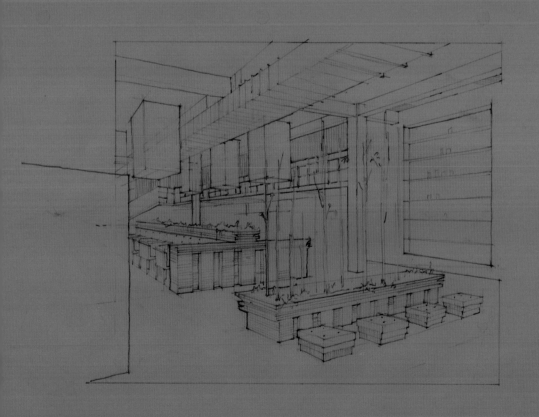

941

SAPA

BANQUE DE

INDO-CHINE

W.282

**Décrets des 21 Janvier 1875,
20 Février 1883, 16 Mai 1900
& 3 Avril 1901**

Emission autorisée le 3 Août 1891

NE PIASTRE | UNE PIASTRE

YABLE EN ESPÈCES | PAYABLE EN ESPÈCES

AU PORTEUR | AU PORTEUR

Administrateur :   *L'Admr-Directeur,*

THE MAKING OF A HILL STATION

The restaurant developed as an experience in which French-inspired design elements would stand independent of Vietnamese-inspired design elements, mirroring the mission of the cuisine. We thought it might be possible to elicit the best of both worlds, not through cultural fusion but through a balanced cultural coexistence of the classic and idiosyncratic patterns and sensibilities so often utilized by artisans and craftsmen of both peoples. From these departure points, the design of Sapa evolved into a study in contrasts—intimate and sweeping, refined and rustic, textured and plain, rough and smooth, indoor and outdoor, East and West.

THERE'S GEOMETRY INVOLVED

Johannes Kepler once wrote that "where there is matter, there is geometry." In attempting to explore juxtaposition through disparity, and materiality through repetition, we were creating formal matter requiring a fair amount of geometry. The long monolithic lines of the bar, the lighting fixtures marching through space, the massive planes of muslin screens, all seem to fit within a seemingly endless orthogonal system of Cartesian coordinates. But this geometric rigor is really only made possible through the structure of the space, literally and figuratively. The existing grid of columns, beams, and ceiling planes set up the staging within which all of the elements of the restaurant could react.

INDUSTRIAL ORGANICS

Industrial geometric forms played a significant role in the architectural design of Sapa, but in each instance they are also contrasted with organic elements. Because we wanted to emphasize the concept of "man-made" vs. "nature-made" it was best to illustrate this contradiction through materials, textures, and the natural lines of the space. For example, the main dining area, from a bit of a distance, looks as if it is dictated by the graceful interaction of industrial lines and materials—the grid of the kitchen windows, appearing somewhat like distant train station windows, the lights that hang in linear order above the bar, and the square steel forms of the custom-made lantern light fixtures. This industrial order is contrasted by the sheer muslin fabrics of the main space partition, a variety of hand-laid woods organically striping the bar surface, and the patterned striations of the natural onyx bar.

Through a stroke of divine luck, the ceiling beams and slabs (formerly hidden) were beautifully gritty, board-formed, cast-in-place concrete. Following the design directive of exploring juxtaposition, we sandblasted and patched the beams as necessary, then added a smooth, whiter than white plaster to the slabs in between. This was inspired by classic old world European ceilings, in which a system of ornate cove and crown plaster moldings would typically surround a central field, often painted with an elaborate narrative. In this case however, the existing rough concrete beams served as our intricate moldings, and the simple white plaster became our minimal narrative.

This contrast between rough and clean is repeated as the beams join the columns. An original part of the structure, these ornately detailed column capitals were in severe contrast to the industrial concrete ceilings, serving as a perfect rift in expectations.

EMULATING NATURE

A number of materials throughout the space were utilized to emulate the patterns found in a natural landscape, albeit a landscape that had been mildly industrialized. We aimed to recreate these elements in both a modern, pragmatic fashion and in a classic decorative way.

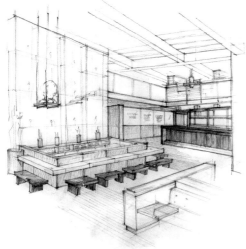

THE ROLL BAR

The Vietnamese roll bar in the center of the restaurant provided a visual anchor to the main dining area, the back dining room, kitchen, and bar. The idea of a glowing monolithic object in the middle of the space was a little too appealing to pass up, so we started to explore white onyx for its natural translucent quality. But the natural veining of the stone was just too overwhelmingly organic and erratic, missing the formal pattern we were searching for. Instead of utilizing the material in a typical application, we designed the bar as a lamination of multiple slabs on end, exposing the sides of the stone instead of their faces. Lights set in the floor flow through the entire bar, exposing cross sections of veins, imperfections, and blemishes, mimicking the striated appearance of bamboo or reed grass.

VILLAGE LIGHTS

Large open spaces can be overwhelming at times; not only do they generally leave little to the viewer's imagination, but they don't offer much variation in experience. Because the existing shell was so grand, Sapa was in danger of being just one cavernous space. To counteract this potential issue, we added a new stair to the cellar as an opportunity to break up the space. Nestling this stair between two, multi-story-high screens behind the Vietnamese roll bar, we were able to both bisect the space on the ground floor as well as provide a compressed yet soaring volume in which to descend the stairs to the lower level. The partitions consist of a delicate steel structure sheathed in layers of sheer white gauze. Light bulbs of varying sizes hang amidst the folds of the fabric, a foray into pattern-making that resembles the lights of a town receding in the distance.

No matter how cavernous and open Sapa was, we still wanted to make every intimate space earn its keep as part of the visual dialogue. Every area was an opportunity to reiterate ideas of intimacy amid the large, sweeping lines of the interior. The staircase behind the Vietnamese roll bar leading to the lower level where the restrooms were located is a perfect example. Too often, these transition spaces are overlooked or treated merely as a stepping-stone from point A to point B. Despite the very small area, we wanted the patrons to feel as if they were walking through a threshold. The sheer partitions spanning both floors allowed for an effortless shift from the main floor, but more importantly, the staircase becomes an experience in of itself; its own space where one can have an intimate, ethereal experience amidst the bustle of the restaurant.

"We developed four iterations of the random pattern the lights would make in the staircase walls, but when we got to the site, the electricians had attempted to give order to the installation, correcting our sketches to get the lights in a perfect line…

"We sometimes take for granted the idea of 'skilled randomization,' as if people should intuit what 'random' might mean in a perfect fashion without much more explanation.

"Euclidian geometry is just so ingrained in most of us. It's human nature to be confused when trying to establish a non-mathematical relationship between 'random' elements."

STAND

The Sapa hostess stand consists of a found antique wooden screen covered in glass and floated above a cast-in-place concrete plinth. Lit from above, the patterns of the screen produce graceful shadows below, in constant motion from the heavy foot traffic.

AND DELIVER

Finding ways to store menus is an ongoing challenge. Often times menus are simply hidden away when not in use, but we try to make them part of the architecture whenever possible, integrated wholly into the look and feel of the space even when they are not in patrons' hands.

As a foray into creating a live decorative pattern, Sapa's menus were designed to stack and sit within a wood screen at the entrance to the restaurant. The bound edges are printed in delicate detail, making a mosaic whose forms change over the course of the night—as the menus are removed from the screen and used, they are inevitably returned to make a new form, a pattern in constant flux with (near) infinite variations.

ONE BAR, FIVE WOODS

A staccato pattern of various species of wood (mostly mahogany, with a sprinkling of cedar, walnut, and whatever was in the shop) makes up the entire bar surface and bar face. The shared, striated visual language of the bar, onyx roll bar and steel handrails all recall decorative strategies utilized in Vietnamese craft. Similar to traditional Vietnamese fabric weaving and furniture making, the inherent character of the source material is never denied; crafts are rarely over-refined or obsessively polished to the point of becoming sterile. Following this ideology, the bar is crafted in similar fashion but with a modern aesthetic. Its monolithic form is only betrayed by a sense of touch, in which the rhythms of the differing wood grains and randomized seams can still be felt, reminding us that despite all the skilled craft, protective sealant, and $15 cocktails that may pass over its surface, it is still a collection of humble, pure and honest pieces of natural wood.

THROUGH THE LOOKING GLASS

In keeping with Sapa's concept of combining controlled, man-made craftsmanship with the organic designs of nature, the large, steel-framed windows dividing the main space from the kitchen were intended to resemble the wrought iron train station windows of the 19th century. The windows, behind which all kitchen activities occur, provide clear separation without the mass and obstruction of an actual wall. The patron does, however, get glimpses of that activity through a few small, strategically placed open windows

FOUND AND FUNCTIONAL

When we come across an object as striking as this wire pulling table, it is hard not to want to find a place for it in a project. Luckily, Sapa was the perfect place to showcase its unique character and detail. A glass surface was added to elevate the height, modernize the piece and add the utility of an extra bar surface. All of the original gears and fittings were kept in place to keep the piece as true to its original form as possible.

"It's an odd object to say the least, strangely agricultural, but actually late 1800s industrial. Its original use wasn't that intuitive and neither was our reuse of it. It took all of two minutes to decide to buy it, but for the life of us, we couldn't figure out why. What's even stranger is that our friend and Project Manager (Chris Larkin) had seen the same table in the market the day before and expected us to purchase it at some point. We think the table just had a curious sense about it."

RESPITE AND RELIEF

Not only was the entire first floor of Sapa already a vast space for us to work with, we also had the luxury of an extremely spacious lower level. It was a rare chance for us to design a slightly excessive number of bathrooms (six), as well as a large common area that could serve as a respite from the intense activity upstairs. With this in mind, we created a massive cast concrete reflecting pool resembling a simple, industrial water trough, the only physical object in this contemplative space. The sole light source on this level emanates from within the pool, creating an austere, meditative atmosphere in stark contrast to the energy and noise of the restaurant above.

Lining one wall of the common area are six identical doors leading to six identical bathrooms. Each door is comprised of ornate wooden screens leading to each bathroom, which is, in turn, completely clad in dado-cut Ipe wood; a modern contrast to the traditional entryway.

"People love the bathrooms at Sapa, but more than three people have told us they thought we were contentious spending so much money planing down and dado-cutting all of the wood cladding for the walls. If they only knew that it's actually just wood flooring applied backwards they'd really start to question the role of architects in modern society."

ALLUSION AND EROSION

Establishing a graphic identity for our projects is always somewhat of a challenge. Since it becomes the visual trademark of the restaurant, it's imperative that the logo and graphics effectively and succinctly convey the brand and mood of the space. Sapa's identity drew inspiration from two primary sources—the intricate patterns and textures of traditional Vietnamese dress and crafts, and a very subtle play on geography. The rough edges of the interwoven patterns suggest a sense of beautiful decay, like an extremely delicate, handmade textile gently fading away with the passage of time. The resulting shapes, while not directly referencing Vietnam's actual coastline, allude to geographic forms in the abstract and exhibit aesthetic traces of antique mapmaking of some mythical locale.

IDENTITY

The identity components—menus, wine lists, etc.—also combine the organic with the synthetic, creating a very tactile experience. The unbleached paper is soft and fiberous and evokes the color and texture of the concrete throughout the space. High-gloss white ink was silk screened and sits beautifully atop the paper, referencing the white glaze of the cast-iron pieces and more polished components of the restaurant. One can feel the actual pattern of the ink on paper.

DESIGN PRINCIPLE
04

UTILITY DRIVEN

When given the opportunity, we aim to make design as utility driven as possible. Every aspect of the architecture, and every object we create goes through a process of Q & A that asks, "How can both patrons and staff use this in the space?" or "How will this object help someone experience the space in a more interactive way?" These types of questions have often pushed us to design beyond the cosmetic (even when cosmetic might have been sufficient), to more layered solutions. This allows those who inhabit the space to become the beneficiaries of more than aesthetics. In doing so, they can actually participate in the function and form of the environment.

THE
E.U.

TURNING THE KITCHEN INSIDE OUT

ALIA AKKAM

While strolling down 4th Street in the East Village, it's hard not to be lured in by E.U.—the striking steel and glass awning, the wide open façade that makes entering this blissful space effortless, the views of the glowing dining room and happily ensconced customers inside. When passersby see the façade's white porcelain-covered bay and catch a glimpse of the kitchen at work, or the garde manger bar extending into the sidewalk, they know that this restaurant encourages dialogue as much as it does honest food.

This harmonious conversation between what's happening on the street in a pulsating city and what's happening on the other side, behind the doors of an innovative yet dependable eatery, is exactly what AvroKO wanted to accomplish. "There is little we aim for more in our restaurant design than a space that can invite you in and then make you feel warm and welcome once inside," says O'Neal. "The open kitchen format, connecting to the outside and the long, windowed street frontage of E.U. gave us this opportunity in spades."

Charged with creating a gastropub, known for its welcoming aura, AvroKO realized they had a sublime model with which to excercise this principle, as it's the gastropub's humble raison d'etre that tends to authenticate the warmth and generosity of its operators. The original gastropubs emerged in London from a simple, distinct necessity—young British chefs needed a place to get started. While the prohibitive cost of renovating London real estate made it difficult for upcoming chefs to lease typical properties, there was a plethora of vacant pubs that had been sold off by breweries after the Beer Orders Act, enacted in 1989 to ensure fair competition between pub operators. Retaining much of their Victorian charm, the advent of these inexpensive empty pubs onto the market coincided with London's gastronomic revolution, becoming a cheap and cheerful option in which chefs with reasonably small budgets could open their own restaurants.

This often meant that whipping up dishes more exotic than bangers and mash led to cramped kitchens, and a restaurant where guests would eat amid no-frills surroundings pieced together by salvaged furniture. Thus the gastropub emerged as a place where diners were treated to a good meal in a charmed ambience. They grew accustomed to this quirky environment where bars were nestled up next to stoves and the chairs they sat on were plucked from a trash bin. Says Farmerie, "Early gastropubs exemplified a modern spirit. The spaces were what they were, and they had an sincere character."

True to the budgetary aesthetics of gastropub culture, AvroKO looked to achieve the same thing with E.U., but with a decidedly unique twist. Using the turn-of-the-century English manor kitchen (both a symbol of household utility and traditional service as a core design reference) they were able to intertwine its key design elements with those of the modern gastropub, based on their common ideals: economy and repurposing ingenuity. Given AvroKO's budget restraints and their knack for taking ordinary objects and giving them new meaning, trips to salvaging sources were frequent. Leave it to them to find undiscovered life in a pile of hickory planks someone was itching to get rid of. Leave it to them to discover that arranging reclaimed turn-of-the-century porcelain tiles in a pattern with cheaper, thinner versions actually accentuates the beauty of the classic finds. This melding of the functional aspects of the gastropub with the design sense of the English manor kitchen essentially meant E.U's concept was simply turning the service elements of the kitchen inside out. According to Bradshaw, "To some degree, it's a lot easier to design restaurants with limited budgets, because ninety percent of the ideas are immediately thrown out the window. However, sometimes finding the other ten percent is like getting water from a stone…but that's also what makes it challenging and fun."

Keeping costs low was paramount, so the key was using the restaurant's raw space to the best of its ability and making way for contemporary touches like hand-blown glass lighting fixtures and a custom porcelain bar. AvroKO also knew that the graphic details couldn't be forgotten, even if they had to be cheap. "We wanted to do something simple and unfussy for the menu design…something that could easily be discarded but would be part of the actual dining experience," says Harris. Brown craft paper menus not only announce what's cooking tonight, but serve as a handsome disposable placemat for the evening….until a fresh one is placed down on the table for lunch tomorrow. Because like many London gastropub regulars, many of the local diners will return the next day, seeking another delicious meal and another set of good laughs.

LET THERE BE LIGHT

This space is located in a tenement build-ing in the East Village, a structure slightly atypical of the kind of apartment buildings generally erected for immigrants in the late 1800s. The property is twice as wide but only half as deep as the standard 16' x 100' downtown NYC lot, making for an unusual amount of street frontage and not a lot of depth.

During demolition, crews concerned about the possibility of damaging supply pipes

pointed out a section of the ceiling in the middle of the space that looked as if it were rotting from years of water damage. When this section was carefully removed, the ceil-ing damage pointed not to leaky water pipes but rather a serendipitous discovery–an internal skylight in disguise. This skylight was in actuality the bottom of a five-story light and air shaft that penetrated through the center of the apartment building above, an old vestige from early NYC building codes enacted to alleviate otherwise congested

tenement housing. (Note: essentially the city required and still requires that each habitable room has a certain number of windows to allow for fresh air and natural light). Normally these shaftways occur at the edges of property lines, but because of this building lot's unusual width we were granted a little luck, as it is extremely rare that a New York restaurant on the first floor of a six-story tenement building could have natural light in the middle of its space.

1. ENTRY

2. HOST

3. GARDE MANGER BAR

4. BAR

5. FRONT DINING

6. BACK DINING

7. RESTROOMS

8. KITCHEN

9. OFFICE

10. PREP KITCHEN

GROUND FLOOR

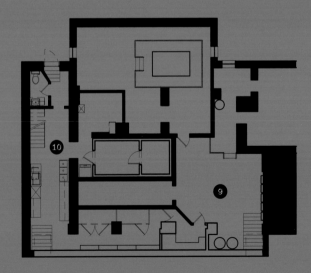

BASEMENT

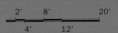

2'　　8'　　20'
4'　　12'

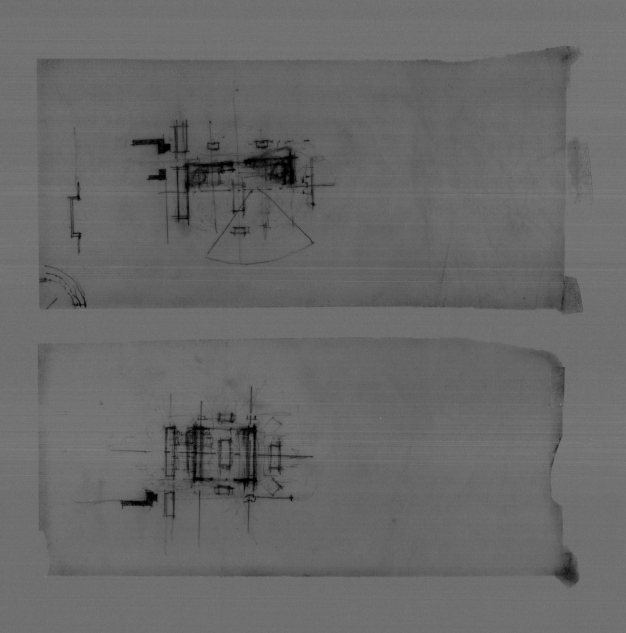

Jeff Koons

137

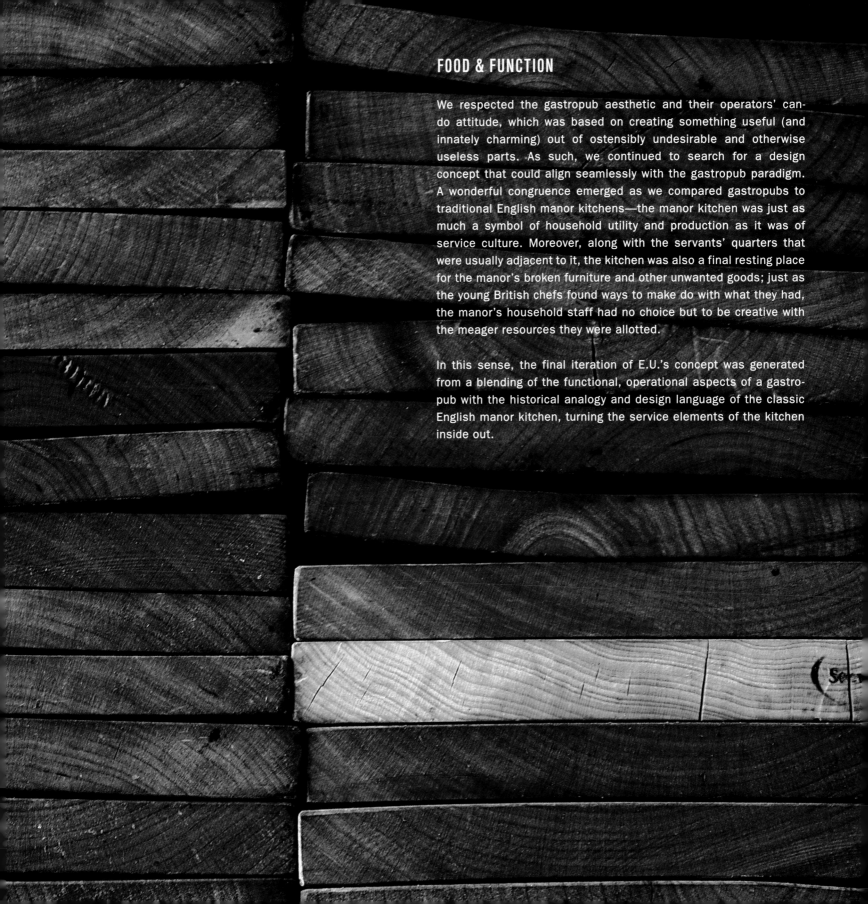

FOOD & FUNCTION

We respected the gastropub aesthetic and their operators' can-do attitude, which was based on creating something useful (and innately charming) out of ostensibly undesirable and otherwise useless parts. As such, we continued to search for a design concept that could align seamlessly with the gastropub paradigm. A wonderful congruence emerged as we compared gastropubs to traditional English manor kitchens—the manor kitchen was just as much a symbol of household utility and production as it was of service culture. Moreover, along with the servants' quarters that were usually adjacent to it, the kitchen was also a final resting place for the manor's broken furniture and other unwanted goods; just as the young British chefs found ways to make do with what they had, the manor's household staff had no choice but to be creative with the meager resources they were allotted.

In this sense, the final iteration of E.U.'s concept was generated from a blending of the functional, operational aspects of a gastropub with the historical analogy and design language of the classic English manor kitchen, turning the service elements of the kitchen inside out.

BLURRING BOUNDARIES

Much of the gastropub's appeal stems from its role as an essential part of the neighborhood landscape, a symbol of comfort and familiarity. It is a place of welcoming, somewhere to gather for a quick drink or linger over a hearty meal. To encourage a comprehensive integration into the community, it was important, then, for E.U. to maintain an open dialogue between the interior and exterior.

We designed the façade in such a way to promote the maximum amount of indoor/outdoor interaction as possible. The first bay of the façade, clad in white porcelain, contains a large kitchen window, which can be left open to receive deliveries and to offer passersby an uncensored glimpse inside a restaurant kitchen in action. The second bay, however, is the best example of how we sought to bring the outdoors in, and vice versa. Two enormous, custom-designed steel casement windows were set on pivoting hinges allowing them to open outward from the inside, opening up the space and creating a glass awning. The monolithic bar/garde manger extends beyond the façade to create an outdoor bar area. Guests may order food and drinks from the convenience of the sidewalk while still maintaining a relationship with the rest of the space through their interaction with the chef manning the counter.

GATHERING THE ORPHANS

The process of finding the chairs for E.U. gave us a good idea of what it might have been like for those new chefs to furnish their gastropubs. Working within the parameters of a limited budget, we set out on another little road trip to Pennsylvania where we visited one of our favorite salvage resources. We needed fifty chairs, but clearly fifty of the same chairs wasn't an option at a salvage warehouse—at best, we could find perhaps a set of five or eight. But having fifty matching chairs would have been antithetical to the gastro-pub concept anyway. The challenge, then, was to curate the huge array of mismatched, discarded chairs and cull it down to the select fifty that were stylistically complementary, with the classic English banking chair as our ideal model. Once we found our fifty, the chairs were stripped down, stained and lacquered to a similar finish, then fitted with a brand new black leather seat cushion. We transformed these somewhat sad, orphaned chairs into a cohesive collection simply by giving them a much-needed makeover.

Return to Client

Clients
Chip →

Return to client

PUSHING PORCELAIN

Dozens of porcelain texture samples were developed
for the E.U. bar from several different manufacturers.
Ultimately we preferred a pristine and unadulterated porcelain to offset much of the other rough and raw materials
in the space. However, our client was very enthusiastic
about experimenting with textures, and we were admit-
tedly curious to see how far we could push the material.
Maybe something really surprising would emerge? After
much exploration, however, the most seductive version
was the first sample created. It was pure, classic, and
true to the material. The client agreed and we proceeded
with the original plan.

PORCELAIN PROSTHETICS

Since we had dismantled the bathroom sinks and supported them with new steel chassis, we had several left over porcelain-glazed cast-iron legs. The two large communal tables' legs currently in the space were fairly unremarkable and not as sturdy as we might have hoped. A swap was in order. The porcelain legs were a perfect height, so off came the wooden legs. A custom wood shoulder was carved to match the exact perimeter of the top of the porcelain. It was stained to match the table and acted as a seamless bridge between two seemingly disparate but ultimately harmonious found objécts.

ONE MAN'S TRASH, ANOTHER MAN'S CEILING

The client wanted to warm up the space and asked if we could incorporate more "woody" elements into the design; with all the porcelain tile work and the concrete floors, he was concerned that the space might start to feel too cold. Our first choice would have been to lay down wood flooring, but in this case, it wouldn't have been an economical choice. Instead, we literally inverted the idea and decided to cover the ceiling in wood, since we could use a much cheaper, unfinished grade. It also made for a much more visually interesting overhead view.

"We took a little road trip with our client out to central Pennsylvania to pay a visit to a man we knew who reclaimed old barns and had some really beautiful old wood. At first we were a little disheartened by the high prices, but then we asked, 'Well, what do you have that you really want to get rid of?' He thought for a moment and then showed us some very old, six inch planks of hickory. Nothing a new stain and some elbow grease couldn't fix, so we bought the whole lot. The man was relieved to see the boards go, and we were relieved to have such a cheap ceiling."

"In order to pull off this unorthodox but potentially beautiful tile installation, we needed to rely again on an artful randomness of placement. Simply instructing the tile setter to have at it and let the tiles fall where they may was probably not a good idea, and the alternative of drawing out in elevation each and every tile was ludicrous. Instead, we laid out a 4'x8' sheet of plywood on saw horses right in the middle of the space and proceeded to play an architecturally demented version of tile dominoes. We created rhythms and standards that seemed to make sense yet still feel random and natural. Once the sheet was covered, we showed it to the installer and said 'Go for it, but all over the place.'"

SOMETHING OLD, SOMETHING NEW

On one of our salvaging trips, we found these incredible reclaimed tiles from the turn of the century. They had been painstakingly glazed by hand, giving each one a unique character. The tiles were too intriguing to pass up, but they weren't cheap. After deliberating about whether or not to splurge on them, we decided to compromise and buy only the amount that would fit into the budget, and then supplement them with newer, more affordable tiles. By juxtaposing the old and new tiles in a random pattern, we were able to draw attention to the beautiful and labored thickness of the vintage tile and thus reveal each's respective manufacturing processes. The vintage tile, at 5/16" thick, had been individually cast in layers, glazed, and sealed; the new tile, by comparison, was only 1/8" thick, their uniformity clearly a result of mass production. The random patterns create a wonderful texture on the walls, while light cast down from above generates compelling shadows and adds depth.

CUTTING IN

Oftentimes in restaurants a vessel of some type is seen resting at the end of the bar, filled with ice and champagne bottles or some other such thing. Our client requested a similar application, but it seemed much too obtrusive to have something that large on top of the bar within this context. Wanting to do something more surprising, we happened upon an old farmhouse sink (porcelain, of course) and loved the idea of marrying the materiality of both porcelain sink and bar, but accentuating the contrast of styles—one clean and modern, the other aged and traditional. Literally insetting the sink within the monolithic plane of the bar heightened this relationship and created a wonderfully quirky, yet highly functional moment.

LOST & FOUND

The Toledo Scale company was founded in 1901 and within five years of its launch, Toledos were appearing on counters and in service kitchens in all parts of the country. Toledo went on to be one of the most recognized utility brand names of the twentieth century...and they were great looking, too. This scale was a perfectly in-tune collaborative contribution from one of the owners, and we were happy to see it arrive. We also learned that thirty-six E.U. side dishes weigh exactly 25 lbs., 8 ozs.

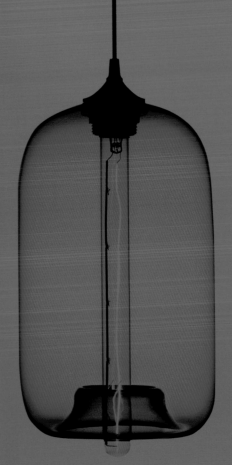

LINE 'EM UP

Showcased in two long rows above the bar, we attempted to elevate the humble serving plate into a modern installation. Made of tin and finished in white enamel, the plates and their repetition create a strong graphic element for this western wall of the space. Slid sideways into individual slots, they are also convenient for the waitstaff to access during busy service hours.

Since E.U. alluded to a number of historical aspects, we were careful to balance that heritage with strong, contemporary moments. While a good deal of the furnishings and accessories sourced for the space were vintage, the lights over the bar add a decidedly modern touch while still maintaining a bit of classic appeal. Their clean, simple shapes contrast nicely with the space without interrupting the integrity of the design.

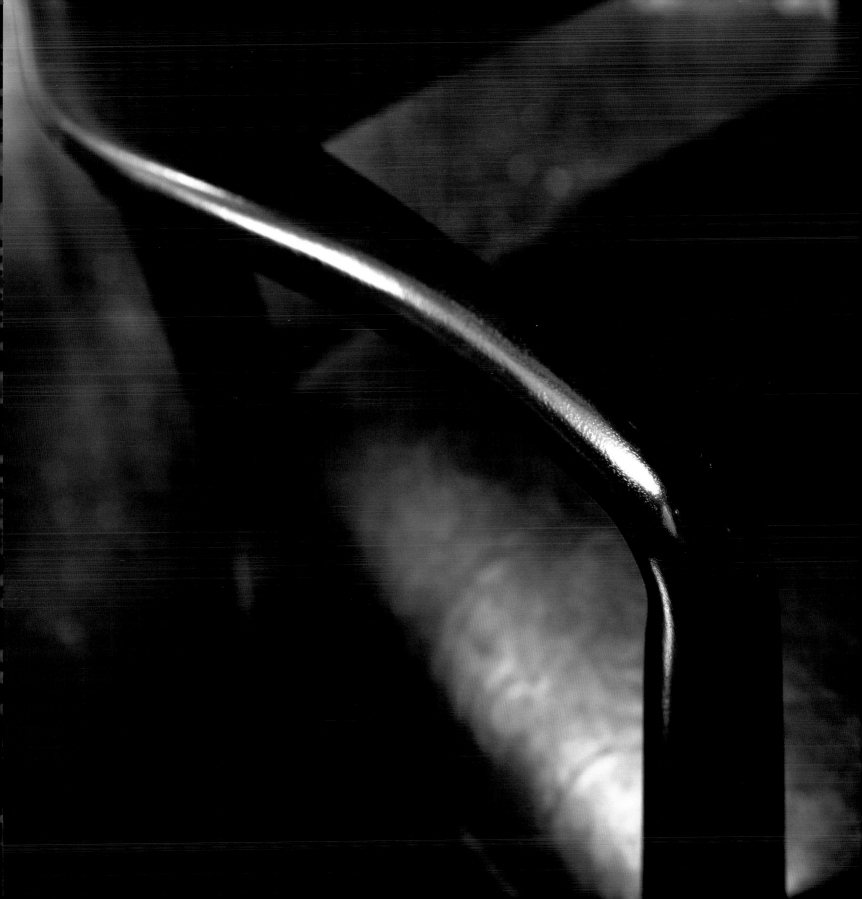

The large wine cabinet at the end of the bar was originally the client's own wine storage from his apartment. It was a large, bulky piece that he thought perhaps could be used in E.U. but wasn't sure how or where. It was actually the very first item that went on-site; as we settled into the construction phase, the contractors moved it to the corner and that's where it stayed for months. After going through multiple rounds of other, more ideal options for wine storage, we eventually ended up coming back to this awkward fellow. After stripping the surface, staining it a rich dark brown, and applying elongated, custom brass pulls, the wine cabinet didn't look so homely after all. In the end, it perfectly echoed the idea of making use of unwanted furniture and giving it a little design love to allow for a new utilitarian life.

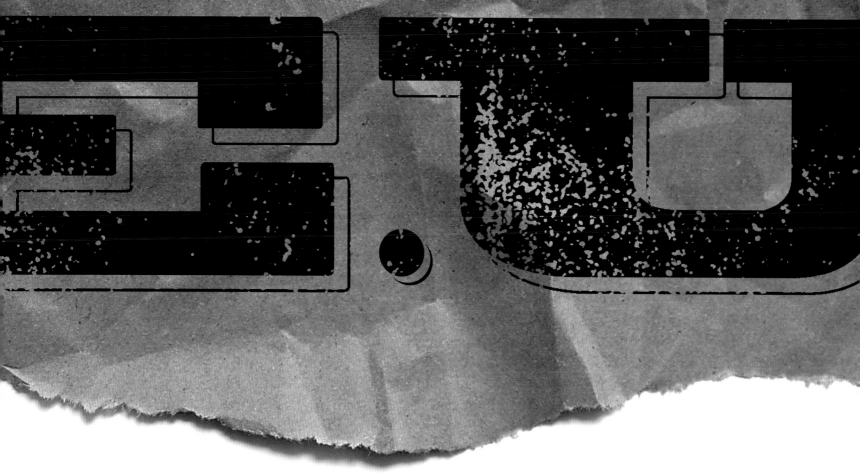

IDENTITY

A humble material was in order for E.U's identity, while a system to integrate it into the main space was also one of our goals. Simple brown craft paper was chosen for its modest and down-to-earth character. Rolls were hung on custom rods mounted to the east wall and served as the raw material for menus. The paper is unrolled, trimmed to size, printed in-house and then serves double duty as placemats. With run of the mill craft paper being as thin as it is, the business cards were offset printed on a much thicker, professional grade stock to match. No one likes a flimsy business card.

THE

E.U.

FOUNDED IN THE BOROUGH OF MANHATTAN

- Butter Clams...$6.00
- Pickled Herring...5.00
- Porcini alla Piastra...$6.00
- Brandade de Morue...$5.00

SANDWICHES ~ PANINI

- Capiocolla Panini w/ Fresh Goat Cheese & Gaeta O
- House-made Pretzel w/ Bauernwurst, Brussel Spro
- Serrano, Manchego & Fig Butter on Semolina Brea

SPECIALS

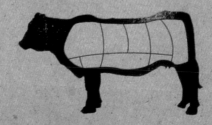

...$9.00

00

Grapes...$9.00

ïoli...$10.00

Gorgonzola...$8.00

se Vinaigrette...$9.00

$8.00

PLATS PRINCIPAUX ~ SECONDS

- Market Fish w/ Winter Savory & Walnut Pesto...$
- Catalonian Lamb "Cassoulet" w/ White Beans & Ga
- House-made Cheese Pumpkin Cavatelli w/ Wild M
- Schnitzle w/ Almond Spaetzle & Pink Pears...$19.0
- Daily Fish & Chips w/ Tartar Sauce & Malt Vineg
- Skate w/ Brown Butter, Apples, & Chestnuts...$20.
- Grilled Bavette Steak w/ Artichoke Gratin...$22.00
- Roast Chicken w/ Red Lentils, Morcilla & Spiced
- Arctic Char w/ Golden Beets, Candied Fennel & L

CHEESE

- Selection of European Artisanal Cheeses:
  $15.00

SIDES ~ ACOMPAÑAMIENTO ~ CONTORNI

- Beer Glazed Carrots..$6.00
- Boiled German Butterball Potatoes...$6.00
- Flat Beans w/ Chorizo...$6.00
- Spaghetti Squash w/ Grana Padana...$6.00
- Pomme Frites & Tomato Aïoli...$6.00
- Roasted Brussel Sprouts & Pancetta...$6.00

SALUMI ~ WURST ~ JAMON

- Pickles, Gnocchio Frito & Olives..$18.00
- Serrano...$6.00
- Prosciutto...$6.00
- Iberico...$6.00

DESIGN PRINCIPLE
#05

SHOW, DON'T TELL

Many of our design concepts are developed from archetypal ideas that have a visceral resonance with us. Translating these ideas into physical architectural elements, however, involves mining each concept until we can "feel" what makes it archetypal and genuine. This process results in a visual storytelling that is manifested in each design element, large and small. Whether the concept involves the confluence of cultures, social institutions, idiosyncrasies of fashion, or even fictional locales in literature, the archetypal notions behind the design become a collection of subtle narratives, combining to create one larger story.

ODEA

THE UNDERBELLY OF SEDUCTION

OLGA KATSNELSON

Odea was AvroKO's follow-up to PUBLIC, and while the latter showed what the team could do when unfettered by client demands, the former was proof positive that they could elegantly overcome a variety of technical and creative challenges with clever innovation. To galvanize the space, AvroKO explored contrasts, pitting refined versus savage, regal versus modest, and dark versus luminous, and thereby transformed—at minimal cost—a small, unforgiving shoebox of a room into a sultry hideaway. Odea forced AvroKO to reexamine their collaborative process. "Initially, we took the spirit of PUBLIC and attempted to shoehorn it into Odea, wanting to oversee every last detail from the interior to the uniforms to the chef," recalls Farmerie. Eventually, they incorporated the client as a team member and collaborator. In this case, the clients were four Little Italy restaurateurs who requested a significant departure from the neighborhood's beloved but tired checkered tablecloth joints, one that ushered in a more contemporary aesthetic.

Seeking the appropriate modern idiom, AvroKO turned to the unexpected source of classical literature, finding fertile ground in Shakespeare's final play. O'Neal recalls, "We ultimately chose *The Tempest* because there was an atmosphere we could create from the intrigue and even mysticism of the story, but it could still be grounded in a real and almost gritty quality." The play follows the shifting fortunes of Prospero, a deposed Milanese duke, who is exiled with his daughter on a mysterious, magical island inhabited by the sprite Ariel and the lustful savage Caliban. AvroKO found a wealth of ideas in imagining the salvaged trappings of nobility—rare books, fine fabrics, and decorative art—mingling with the cruder landscape of an untamed island.

AvroKO elevated the cave-like metaphor of the space to its stylistic, urban realization, taking a cue from Caliban's penumbral lair and playing up the inherent darkness. A "palate" of blacks was called for, but not just any black would do; AvroKO insisted on locating and testing a range of blacks until the proper qualities of black were hit upon. This darkened interior also allowed AvroKO a rich exploration of textures and fabrics for the right invocations of mood—resulting in the buttery black leather covering the banquette in the lounge, the tufted black silk pillows tossed about the sofas, and the black satin embossed with diamonds and crests animating the backbar.

The effect of this intended darkness is not unlike that of walking into a Gothic cathedral where, amidst the shadows, any light source registers like a dazzling explosion. The luminous bar area at the entrance makes a striking first impression. The amber onyx bar top, lit from below so its crimson veins emerge from a pale gold background, appears to float on air. The backbar features rows of niches, each one softly lit to offset a stark white marble bust, dramatically lit against the black background. Further inside, the chiaroscuro effect is generated by a constellation of twinkling votive candles and spherical glass chandeliers.

Another challenge was the client's request for a lounge area, a concept requiring far more horizontal space than was available.

As a solution, AvroKO accessed the vertical space, creating a series of raised platforms on which three semi-private niches, each accommodating up to fifteen people, are situated. Master scavengers and re-appropriators, AvroKO transformed inexpensive raw-timber planks, normally used to hold back dirt in construction sites, into the sultry walls of the lounge areas.

The client also wanted to accommodate dining. As adding dining tables would have cluttered the lounge niches, AvroKO played up an indulgent, more casual atmosphere of feasting on finger foods and shared plates, obviating the need for formal place settings and tables. They created disarming, seductive spaces that accommodate both dinner and cocktail hour. Black wooden ottomans perform double duty as mini dining tables or additional seating. Cascading, semi-transparent muslin curtains can be drawn by guests craving further seclusion and giving the restaurateurs the option to book semi-private parties. The only decoration is a gilt-framed mirror with proportions straight out of a fairy tale, creating a focal point for the entire back area.

With Odea, AvroKO asserted the breadth of their collective imagination and the depth of their technical expertise. Expertly navigating around the potential for unfortunate clichés that a Shakespearean theme can bestow, they showed their skill for evoking a mood, pleasing a client, and creating, in the words of *The Tempest*'s Miranda, a "brave new world."

LITTLE ITALY NORTH

When we were first approached by our clients, we were excited to do another project near NoLIta, a neighborhood in downtown New York where both PUBLIC and our offices are located. The four owners of this new bar/lounge had all grown up just south of us in Little Italy, and while their neighborhood was once rich in tradition and culture, it now had given way to more cookie-cutter red sauce joints and souvenir stands. In response to the touristy development of the neighborhood, they collectively wanted to introduce something with more character, just off the main Mulberry Street stretch.

As with many of our projects, we learned that the existing space had an extremely interesting history. It was originally built to house a local winery called Aquino; grapes were actually delivered straight from Italy, and arrived at the site via a gantry built on the roof. The grapes were then lowered through holes in the roof to the upper level, where they were basket pressed and gravity fed (the upper floors were built on an incline) directly into barriques on the ground floor for fermentation. The winery had been built for a family that reportedly had to leave Italy under inauspicious circumstances, and

there was something at once heroic and tragic about this enterprise: banished Italian immigrants searching for a new beginning in America, only to import their country's natural resources in order for them to work as they did at home.

The idea of Prospero escaping persecution with nothing but his daughter and his books became a fun and romantic (although completely coincidental) analogy to the original family of the Aquino winery.

1. ENTRY

2. HOST

3. BAR

4. SEATING AREA 1

5. SEATING AREA 2

6. SEATING AREA 3

7. WOMEN'S RESTROOM

8. MEN'S RESTROOM

9. KITCHEN

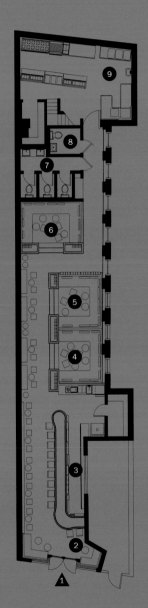

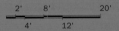

2'   8'   20'
   4'   12'

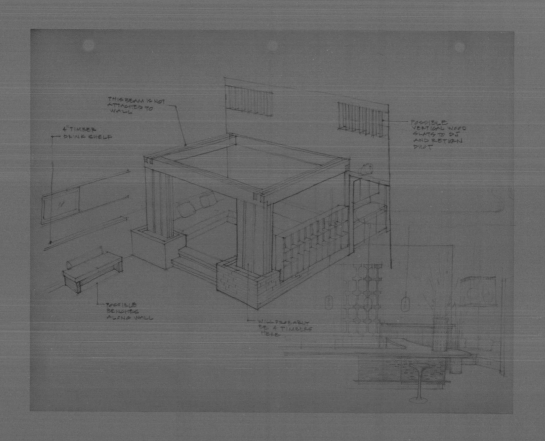

THIS BEAM IS NOT
ATTACHED TO
WALL

4" TIMBER
DINING SHELF

POSSIBLE
VERTICAL WOOD
SLATS TO D.J
AND RETURN
DUCT

POSSIBLE
BENCHES
ALONG WALL

WILL PROBABLY
BE 4 TIMBERS
TABLE

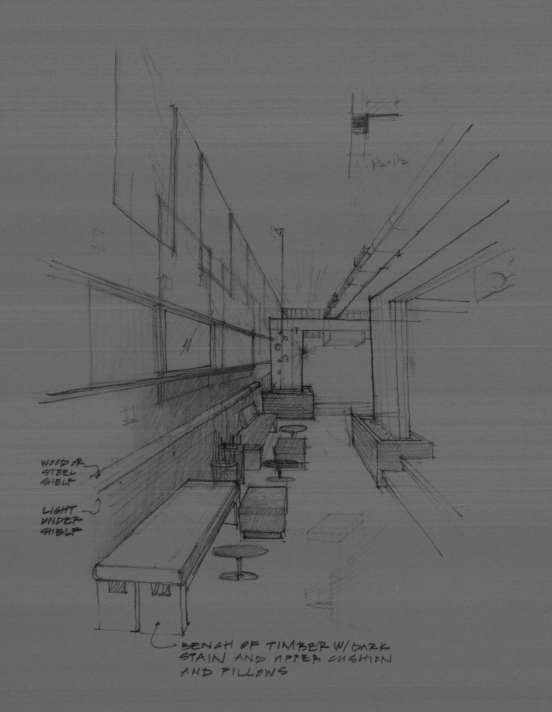

WOOD OR
STEEL
SHELF

LIGHT
UNDER
SHELF

BENCH OF TIMBER W/ DARK
STAIN AND UPPER CUSHION
AND PILLOWS

1¼-1½

DRAMATIS PERSONÆ.

ALONSO, *King of Naples.*

SEBASTIAN, *his brother.*

PROSPERO, *the right Duke of Milan.*

ANTONIO, *his brother, the usurping Duke of Milan.*

FERDINAND, *son to the King of Naples*

GONZALO, *an honest old Counsellor.*

ADRIAN,
FRANCISCO, } *Lords.*

CALIBAN, *a savage and deformed Slave.*

TRINCULO, *a Jester.*

STEPHANO, *a drunken Butler.*

Master of a Ship.

Boatswain.

Mariners.

MIRANDA, *daughter to Prospero.*

ARIEL, *an airy Spirit.*

IRIS,
CERES,
JUNO, } *presented by Spirits.*
Nymphs,
Reapers,

Other Spirits attending on Prospero.

The Tempest.

Act First.

Scene I.

On a ship at sea : a tempestuous noise of thunder and lightning heard.

Enter a Ship-Master and a Boatswain.

Mast. Boatswain !

Boats. Here, master : what cheer ?

Mast. Good, speak to the mariners : fall to 't, yarely, or we run ourselves aground : bestir, bestir.   [*Exit.*

Enter Mariners.

Boats. Heigh, my hearts ! cheerly, cheerly, my hearts ! yare, yare ! Take in the topsail. Tend to the master's whistle. Blow, till thou burst thy wind, if room enough !

Enter Alonso, Sebastian, Antonio, Ferdinand, Gonzalo,

A TEXTURED TALE

Despite Odea's monochromatic color scheme, or perhaps because of it, the space really taps into a person's sensual experience. While it's not immediately perceived visually, a certain tactile sensuality is achieved throughout the space from the application of various textures—the slate walls, upholstery fabrics, smooth stones, rough timbers, and matte ceramics, all of which coexist in tones of black or deep charcoal. Because they follow similar hues, these materials rely on their respective textures and contours to absorb, reflect, or refract light to articulate the space. With one's visual field handicapped to some degree, the remaining senses become heightened and dominate a larger part of our perception. The minimal color palette allows patrons to fully experience the guttural bass of the music, the sweet smell of beeswax, and the sensual touch of silk, thus creating a sexy, alluring atmosphere not only through what is visually apparent, but also through what can be felt and heard.

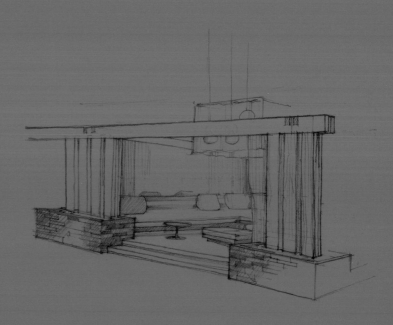

A beautiful tension and a compelling story can be constructed when contrasting gritty roughness with graceful refinement. Much like the primitive imagined landscape of Shakespeare's mystical island and the exiled royalty that roamed it, Odea balances raw and natural materials like rough-hewn timbers and dark stone with more sumptuous items like silks and ornately hand-carved wood mirrors.

183

A SELECTION OF PROSPERO'S BOOKS

There are twenty-four books that Gonzalo hastily threw into Prospero's boat as he was pushed out into the sea to begin his exile from Milan. These books enabled Prospero to find his way across the oceans, to combat the malignancies of Sycorax, to colonize the island, to free Ariel, to educate and entertain Miranda, and to summon tempests bringing his enemies to heel. While we used *The Tempest* as an overarching reference, we had not intended to literally recreate every element from the narrative; however, there are some curious and delightfully apropos parallels to Prospero's books that became apparent in the design.

BOOK #4
A PRIMER OF THE SMALL STARS

Amber-lit globes hover in a cluster over every den as both interpretations of celestial mystery and references to Renaissance chandelier forms.

BOOK #6
A HARSH BOOK OF GEOMETRY

Varying lengths and widths of rough-cut black slate catch the candlelight while maintaining a sense of weight and rough organic form.

BOOK #2
A BOOK OF MIRRORS

The detail and care put into this hand-carved wood framed mirror recalls the craftsmanship of "civilization" and the comforts of an aristocratic home.

BOOK #20
LORE OF RUINS

Raw and beautifully decrepit, this weathered brick was an artifact of the original space and a perfect backdrop for the design.

BOOK #18
THE AUTOBIOGRAPHIES OF PASIPHAE AND SEMIRAMIS

Black tufted silk pillows add a luxurious and regal touch, while alluding to sensuality and sexuality.

BLACK ON BLACK ON BLACK ON BLACK

PROSPERO'S BOOK # 7: THE BOOK OF COLORS

"This is a large book bound in crimson watered silk. It is broader than it is high, and when opened the double-page spread makes a square. The three hundred pages cover the color spectrum in finely differentiated shades moving from black back to black again . . ."

For this project, we set out to find the perfect black. Not just any black, but *the* black. One might be surprised that a fair amount of energy would go into this endeavor; technically, black is either the absence of color (as in light), the combination of all color (as in paint), or simply a variable firing of neurons stimulated from the ganglion (in neurology). Nevertheless, we were just not satisfied with the stream of different black paints that we tested—this one was too gray, that one had a hint of red. We could have settled on whatever we found at the local paint shop, but that would be entirely antithetical to the process, and not nearly as fun, frustrating, or satisfying.

"We went through over twenty-four test mixtures of paint, painted a strip of each on the wall in sections, and went back to the drawing board again to get the perfect sheen. Needless to say, the painting subcontractor didn't find this process as intriguing as we did.

"The paint was just reacting to different materials in different ways, as it tends to do, so we were constantly remixing the blacks to make sure they felt the same no matter what surface they were on or what surface they were next to...sort of a Joseph Albers color theory study, but with no color. Essentially, none of the variations were truly working as far as we could tell.

"Someone suggested we make a lateral shift to white paint half way through the process, which was not that well received."

GETTING WAXED

We knew of a place out in Brooklyn that had these great, heavy wood timbers that were cheap. We could say that these were inexpensive, but that's giving them too much credit...they were just cheap. In actuality, these timbers were typically used in street excavation, creating temporary walls to hold back dirt—not exactly glamorous. But we were able to look beyond their prescribed usage and found a rough beauty in them, and proceeded to go through with what seemed an endless series of tests with one of the woodworkers. After trying any twelve-step process we could think of, we eventually realized the answer was in a can of black gorilla wax. A red stain applied first peeks through just enough in the deeper grain to give the material a depth we couldn't have anticipated.

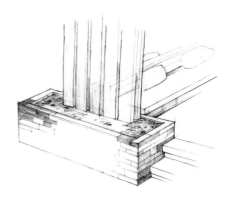

SEX AND EXILE

With *The Tempest* as our muse, we hoped to elicit the same passionate emotions that existed at the heart of the play—raw desire, repressed lust, intrigue. The primitive aspect of the island is illustrated in the timbers and slate used in the back part of the lounge, but it is the exoticism of the huge under-lit onyx bar that brings an almost magical element to the space. The contradictory nature of both areas creates a contrast between the base and the refined, much like the tension between the underworld of Caliban and the cultured and regal worlds of Miranda and Prospero.

METAPHORS AND MATERIALITY

The purity and beauty of natural materials can be manipulated to varied effect. The inherent undulation of the veins and color variations in Odea's honey onyx bar was accentuated by lighting under its surface. Here, the resulting glow of the stone acts as both a main lighting element welcoming patrons into the space as well as a conceptual reference point; its graphically organic quality an allusion to the natural elements of the fictional island.

PATTERN PLAY

The wall behind the backbar, hidden behind a myriad of liquor bottles, glasses, shelves and casement, is an area that is typically overlooked or surrendered to budget cuts and "value engineering" exercises. It's often an uncelebrated part of any bar, namely because so little of it is seen. In Odea's case, we knew the low light would be an opportunity to show off the more layered and visually rich architectural moment that the backbar became...another foray into black on black of course. The faintest texture is visible, a diamond-patterned fabric with classic crest fleur de lis. The diamond motif hints at a regal heritage, while the nominal variations in color hue and sheen add an additional depth to the already receded surface. The result is that the plane of the backbar seems to be almost infinite.

KEEPING SENTINEL

One of the more noted objects of Odea, only slightly overshadowed by the massive, glowing onyx bar, are the various ceramic busts that occupy the oval grid of shelves at the backbar. They are formally arresting (being the only white objects in the space), but they add a curious human element as well. The busts have a haunting quality and a tragic beauty in this context, the vacuous representation of figures from a mythical utopia.

COMMUNITY VS. PRIVACY, OR A LITTLE BIT OF BOTH

In order to give our clients operational flexibility, we often love to toy with the idea of a space within a space, and a lounge is really an ideal venue to experiment with this concept.. The three distinct, elevated areas were designed to entertain communal experiences, while the translucent sheer curtains that close them off provide the ability to promote a number of sensations somewhere between privacy and mischief.

A STUDY IN CONTRASTS

The graphic identity for Odea is a two-dimensional embodiment of the project's architectural points of departure. As the design direction of the space was based on both a monochromatic color scheme and a texture-intense experience, envisioning the identity for Odea turned out to be a very fluid process.

Having explored numerous relationships of duality and contrast throughout the space, it was only natural that we would settle on black and white for the identity. An extremely tactile and very curious rubberized paper was used to wrap the exterior of the menu. The matte surface material is so black and so dense that it absorbs any light that comes across it. To further increase this sensation, we screen printed the logo and exterior graphics in high gloss white and gold inks, while the interior was covered in an ornately patterned spot varnish, a direct play on the fabric behind the bar. The letterhead, a warm white, is framed in a dense black frame, reminding one that even though there may be pragmatic moments of lightness, Odea is always, always ensconced in black.

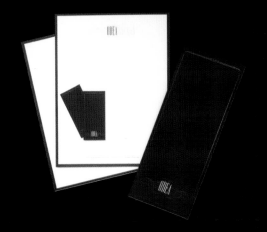

food

Spicy Almond Candy
caramel with an array of spices

Eggplant Mousse
Sesame paste, roasted garlic and grilled bread

Picholin Olives
stuffed with boccaronne and roasted peppers

Fresh Figs
wrapped with prosciutto finished with a citrus drizzle

Pave of Grilled Eggplant
with tomato confit and feta cheese

Grilled Shrimp and Pineapple
with tamarind sauce

Smoked Paprika Flat Bread
wild mushroom, nigella, garoxata cheese,
and pickled pearl onion

Baby Green Salad
watermelon, feta cheese, spicy croutons and pistachio dressing   8

Kubë
with beef, mint, cucumber, and lime raita   8

Butternut Squash Gnocchi
fresh ricotta, Vermouth, basil and shallot confit   9

Danish Baby Ribs
with an asian dipping sauce and watercress
and green apple salad   9

Crispy Baby Squid
yellow chili and saffron aïoli, garlic harrisa   10

e Cevichë
hee, purple basil, lime and fresh Thai peppers   11

allop
, vanilla tomato confit, fennel salad   11

Skirt Steak
d cabrales blue cheese   12

Jennel   15

                                                                                   16

ODEA

DESIGN PRINCIPLE

#06

ORDERING THE ORDINARY

A mundane object can be made compelling simply by rearranging its placement, context and/or quantity to give it new meaning. Sometimes we are able to do this through repetition, creating form and pattern, which is really a traditional design vehicle...and we can't think of any designer who hasn't implemented this method at some time or another. The more interesting twist we prefer to employ includes juxtaposing modern and vintage material combinations to give an object a completely new form that was not remotely intended by its maker. There is always fun in this type of interplay and it can turn the perception of an object on its ear.

SAFE HANDLING INSTRUCTIONS
THIS PRODUCT WAS PREPARED FROM INSPECTED AND PASSED
MEAT AND/OR POULTRY. OUR BEEF IS STORED IN DEDICATED
MEAT LOCKERS AT A CONSTANT 34 DEGREES FAHRENHEIT.

THE CONSTANT FLOW OF AIR RESULTS IN A
DARK PATINA ON THE SURFACE OF THE MEAT AS
WELL AS GREAT TENDERNESS AND RICHER
FLAVOR IN THE RESULTING STEAKS.

COOK
THOROUGHLY.

THROUGHOUT THE AGING PROCESS, AMINO
ACIDS ARE RELEASED THAT BREAK DOWN THE
MUSCLE FIBERS IN THE STEAK, RESULTING IN
NATURALLY TENDERIZED MEAT WITH
CONCENTRATED FLAVORS.

KEEP HOT FOODS HOT.
REFRIGERATE LEFT-
OVER IMMEDIATELY
OR DISCARD.

QUALITY MEATS

OLD MEATS NEW

JAY CHESHES

Quality Meats represents a departure, geographically and otherwise, from AvroKO's earlier restaurant work. The modern steakhouse is in midtown Manhattan, far from the downtown locale where they forged their reputation. It also marked the beginning of a new working relationship with the Smith & Wollensky Group, in which Quality Meats became a sort of prototype for bringing the firm's distinctive design imprint to a much wider audience.

The unlikely partnership began with a visit to PUBLIC. Wollensky Group CEO Alan Stillman had been tossing around ideas for updating his brand when his son Michael lured him downtown to the AvroKO owned and designed restaurant. The excursion gave way to a lunch meeting with the AvroKO team and a few months later they were in business together. "We started talking about this new concept, a national venture," recalls Harris. "And then they slipped in, 'By the way, we have this other little restaurant and it kind of needs a little something. It's twenty-two years old, it was great in its heyday, but it's time for something else to happen.'"

The "little restaurant" in question was the Manhattan Ocean Club, a clubby seafood spot just south of Central Park. AvroKO was offered three months to transform the dated all-white space from a sort of terrestrial ocean liner into an industrial steakhouse, completely erasing all vestiges of the original. The results are as remarkable for the totality of the vision as the timetable in which it all came together. The team tackled every aspect of the metamorphosis,

beginning with the restaurant's new name and working their way down to tabletop, uniforms, matchbooks, and menus. Initial inspiration came from their corporate partner themselves. The whitewashed Quality Meats sign in the restaurant's front bar room is a classic butcher shop icon that hangs in all eleven Smith & Wollensky steakhouses.

The name gave rise to the overall design concept they eventually pursued. "We asked ourselves, 'Does the world really need another steakhouse?'" recalls Bradshaw. "How can we do something a little more interesting and surprising?" They found their answer at Albanese Meats, a no-frills butcher shop just up the block from the AvroKO studio. A time-warp relic on a block now teeming with fashion boutiques, the cluttered storefront became the launching pad for the general mood at Quality Meats. "Nothing's ever really a direct pull," said O'Neal. "Mostly it's playing with variations of an original idea... We particularly enjoyed the romanticism of the old-world New York butcher shop as a concept."

The AvroKO team has an intuitive knack for turning workaday objects and concepts into dramatic design touches. Materials first spotted in a neighborhood butcher shop were repurposed in the restaurant in ingenuous ways—butcher block was transformed into sills and stairs, screw patterns picked up from the inside of a meat locker showed up on the dining room walls, classic white ceramic tiles covered a long curving wall at the entrance.

The space, meanwhile, lost layers—and years—of drywall and paint. The hidden substructure became a focal point for the new design. Exposed beams and slabs of concrete lend the finished product a gritty industrial edge. "We definitely respect and celebrate some methods of construction that at times aren't meant to be seen," said Farmerie. "They're pure and functional and in some ways very modern."

Layered with the butcher materials and other found objects, the dining room itself carries an understated menace. The ironic sense of foreboding—this is, after all, a restaurant devoted to the consumption of big hunks of meat—is further heightened by design elements like an upstairs art installation using wall-mounted meat cleavers. The most striking of these AvroKO inventions is a light fixture fashioned from meat hooks that have been sandblasted and nickel-plated.

In the end Quality Meats is an urban steakhouse unlike any other—combining a modern sensibility with materials that channel a slower-paced, vanished New York. It's just what Stillman and son had in mind when they took a leap of faith, authorizing the demolition of the Manhattan Ocean Club without any concrete plans on paper (many of the working blueprints, scribbled on sheetrock during construction, are now hidden in the finished restaurant). "Until this restaurant was completed everyone in the company had been looking at me like I was insane," said Michael Stillman. "Suddenly they started to get it."

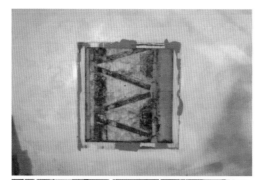

ERASING A BRAND

For over twenty-two years, the Manhattan Ocean Club—an upscale, midtown staple for $90 seafood towers and pin-striped power lunches—occupied a prime slice of real estate near Sixth Avenue just below Central Park. The M.O.C., as it was affectionately dubbed, enjoyed its heyday and instant name recognition during the booming eighties through the nineties, but the owners (the Smith & Wollensky Restaurant Group) felt it was time for a change.

The initial directive from our client was to keep things simple: slap on a new paint color,

reupholster the chairs, install new lights in the same location as the existing ones, and maybe stain the floors. The other half of their directive was that they wanted no recognition of the M.O.C. as it was formerly known, so completely erasing a well-known brand was going to require far more drastic measures.

After several discussions, and a giant leap of faith from the client, it was apparent that we needed to bring out the heavy equipment and tear the existing space apart. With only three months from the time the M.O.C. doors closed to the Quality Meats doors opening,

a truly mercenary approach would be necessary. Armed with the knowledge that this building, originally erected in 1910, would probably have some inherent characteristics to salvage (but still with our fingers slightly crossed), we watched as demolition crews started pulling down dropped acoustic ceilings, millwork cladding at columns, and gypsum board furring at party walls. Pay dirt. When the dust cleared, we were relieved to see that there was enough uniqueness to the existing architecture with which to ground a new design.

1. ENTRY

2. HOST

3. CHARCUTERIE BAR

4. LOUNGE

5. BAR

6. DINING 1

7. DINING 2

8. DINING 3

9. DINING 4 (PRIVATE)

10. PHONE ROOM

11. WOMEN'S RESTROOM

12. MEN'S RESTROOM

13. KITCHEN

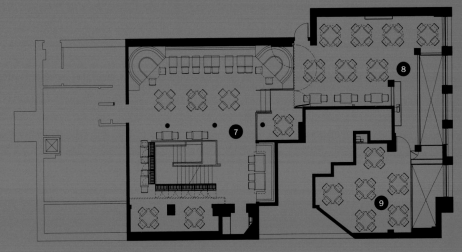

SECOND FLOOR

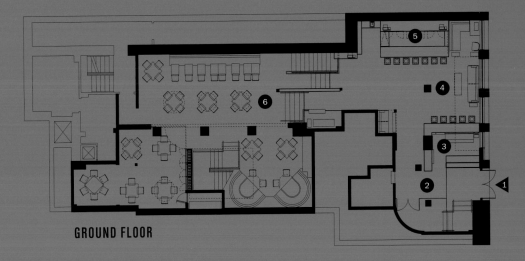

GROUND FLOOR

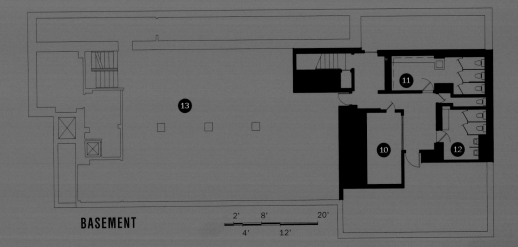

BASEMENT

2'   8'   20'

4'   12'

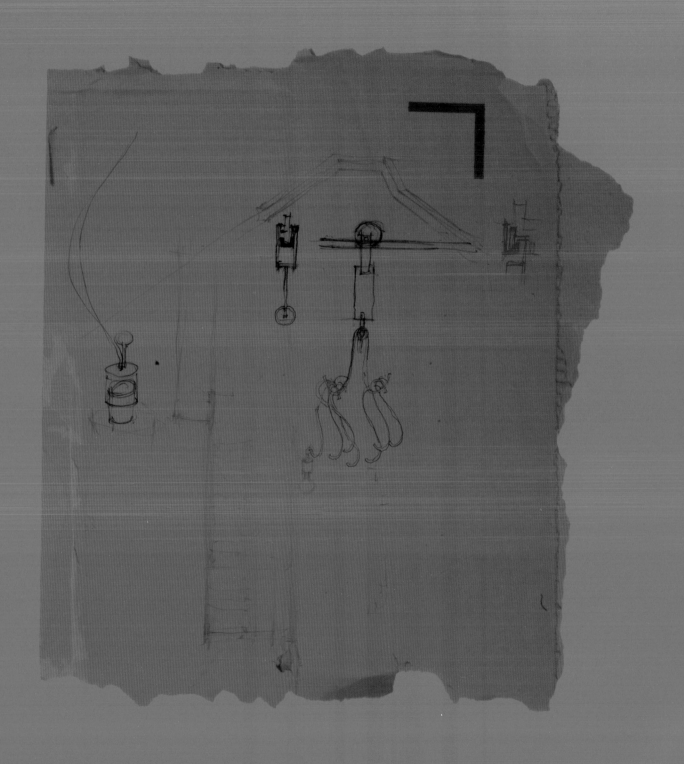

208

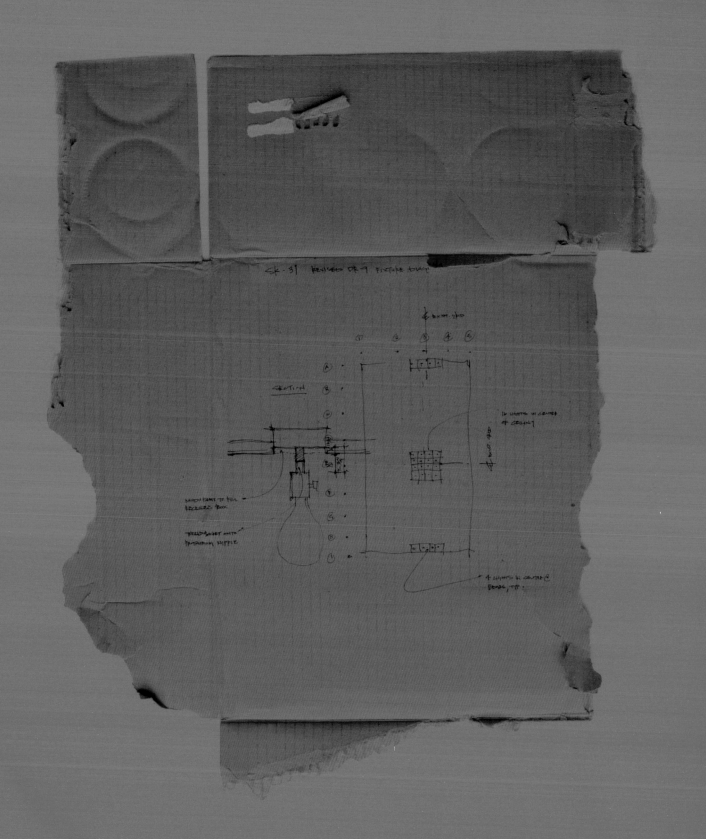

ODE TO THE OLD WORLD

On our way to work, we would often pass by a storefront a block away from our offices on Elizabeth Street that, despite massive development and modern shops around it, still had the charm of the old neighborhood butcher shop. This was Albanese Meats, a tiny family-owned business that had been operating for nearly ninety years in a neighborhood that was fast becoming dominated by designer boutiques and luxury condos. Every time we walked by we couldn't help but to peer in and wonder about this indispensable staple of the community. When Quality Meats came onto the boards, the urge to step inside and poke around became unbearable.

We ultimately met Mo Albanese (pictured left), the extremely likeable and slightly sassy proprietor of Albanese Meats. He generously explained his family and butcher shop history, as well as an account of this neighborhood in which they had all been raised, to our rapt attention. He introduced us to his friends and neighbors at small gatherings in the butcher shop, where cut-off bits of meat were cooked up on the spot and the wine he made in the basement flowed freely. He allowed us to poke around in century-old meat lockers and peruse his dozens of family photos documenting the many generations. The visual and emotional experiences we shared here became the basis of our inspiration for Quality Meats.

"Albanese Meats and the family-owned building it's in is dripping with history. According to Mo, Martin Scorcese cut his first film above the butcher shop, and many of the neighborhood regulars who linger around the shop have been cast in his other films. Apparently, everyone in the neighborhood is an 'actor.' When we asked if we could take his photo one day, Mo asked if he'd get 'rate,' referring to his SAG (Screen Actor's Guild) membership. Absolutely brilliant.

"We made the mistake of bringing Brad, the chef at PUBLIC, to one of Mo's gatherings at the shop. Now, every time we stop by to say hello, he only wants to know two things from us: 1) when is Kristina coming over again, and 2) when is Brad going to put in another order for lamb's neck?"

COVERED IN BLOOD, BUT STILL STYLISH

There's no better sign of respect for one's craft than dressing smartly while performing it, especially if that craft is inherently a bit on the messy side. We loved the numerous images we came across during our research of turn-of-the-century butcher shops, of butchers wearing stylish ties, cardigans, felt fedoras, and even pocket squares at times while heartily carving into a bloody side of beef. Perhaps this stylishness and attention to detail was simply a sign of more sincere times, but it certainly resonated with us, serving as inspiration for the waiters' uniforms at Quality Meats.

THE FIGURE HEAD

When we spotted a bull's head sculpture from Smith & Wollensky's collection of antique Americana, it seemed a perfect opportunity to indulge in creating a somewhat post-modern element at the entrance of Quality Meats. Cast of aged white plaster, the object situates itself well among the sea of off-white ceramic tiles, which were installed with an exaggerated horizontal grout line to accentuate the curve of the entrance wall. The head pokes out of a white laminate-lined niche and recalls, to some extent, turn-of-the-century signage techniques where images or carvings symbolizing a particular shop's wares were displayed in place of text, to ensure that the community's predominantly illiterate masses knew what the shop was selling.

The monochromatic color scheme throughout the entry sequence is a nod to various butcher shop accoutrements—fresh white wax paper, slick white marble counters, white linen butcher jackets—and the means with which to immediately encase the visitor in a thoroughly modern context despite the confluence of historically disparate elements.

"The bull's head came to us from the Las Vegas Smith & Wollensky's with tiny hand signatures scribbled all over it; seemingly the accrued graffiti from a number of years in service. After we spotted it in a blurry photograph, they literally took it off the wall for us and sent it to New York. A lot of consideration went into whether we should keep the head in the condition it had arrived or whether we should sand away some of its history, including the signatures, for a more pristine look...

"At first we were excited by the signatures, and imagined that they were quite old and had been scrawled onto this bull's head over the past hundred years (as they were kind of hard to make out at first glance). But once we realized that they were from some event in the early '90s, we immediately decided to remove them despite the risk we took in damaging the object. A scrawled signature by Carmello Calandruccio from 1918 would have been interesting; whereas a sprightly signature with hearts dotting the i's by Jenni Smith in marketing was decidedly less so."

THE MATERIAL CHOICE OF A PAST GENERATION

Due to its association with uses in early medical offices, operating theaters, and other typically sanitary applications, and despite its porous nature and need for maintenance, marble may be one of the single most ubiquitously used materials in the quintessential butcher shop. White Carrera marble from Italy, to be specific, was often the stone of choice: beautifully pure and pristine, with gorgeous but subtle gray veins not unlike the marbling in a perfectly dry-aged steak.

PRIMED

The first experience a visitor encounters after entering Quality Meats is the charcuterie bar, in spatial opposition to the drinks bar, offering tasty cuts of cured meats along with cheeses, homemade potato chips, and mostardas. The Ferrari of meat slicers, the Berkel Mito 300 sits front and center in all of its candy apple red glory. Jars of molasses, honey, and salt are stored on glass and steel shelves along the back bar, within handy reach should the charcuterie bar chef decide to do some on-the-fly meat curing during service.

Absolutely the biggest drawbacks and design hurdles to be negotiated from the original M.O.C space were the oppressively low ceiling heights at the entry and bar areas, a whopping seven feet, four inches. How this restaurant had operated like this for twenty-two years was beyond us, as the minimum ceiling heights for habitable spaces as dictated by the New York City Department of Building Code is seven feet, six inches. They were two inches short of ceiling heights usually reserved for basements! Needless to say, the space felt slightly claustrophobic.

WHEN ARE YOU GOING TO FINISH THE CEILING?

Obviously, something had to be done. We removed several of the dropped acoustic ceiling panels, and above the rat's nest of electrical wiring and insulated ducting, appeared to be a gorgeous board formed concrete structure some four-teen inches higher than what the restaurant was currently living with. It was a no-brainer; gain the desperately needed ceiling height and a beautiful ceiling surface in one fell swoop. A quick assessment of how to run new exposed duct and re-routed electrical conduit seemed to work cleanly, so we began a hard lobby to pull down all of the existing ceilings. After some heavy coaxing, the client agreed despite grave reservations that exposed board formed concrete may not be as beautiful as we claimed.

"As the project was nearly finished, every time one of us would walk through the space the staff would ask 'when are you going to finish the ceilings?'"

"Having spent most of the project on site, we had the pleasure of hearing this nearly every day for three months; from our clients, from their employees, even from random passersby. We developed an automatic response that we had hoped was a pleasant smile but was probably more like a neurotic twitch."

SUPPORT SYSTEM

One of our favorite finds when the space was demolished was the incredible concrete and steel columns throughout the first floor. Once concealed by layers of plaster and paint, the construction of the columns—rough concrete framed by welded steel trusses—was more remarkable than anything we could have imagined. We later learned that this construction encased the original cast-iron columns, which was considered curious even by our structural engineer's standards. The steel truss was adhered in the 1970s to bolster the existing structure so that a second floor could be added, with the concrete acting to bind the inner original and outer new columns together.

BUTCHER'S BLOCK

There is a fine line between exploring "inspiration" and replicating it. Trying to refrain from making anything too overt, our efforts are generally concentrated on appropriating visual elements and implementing them in modern translations. The use of end grain wood flooring to elicit a sense of traditional end grain butcher blocks is a good example of this principle in action. Used mainly as flooring in transition areas (including the main staircase), it was the ideal material for heavy traffic—a wood's end grain is its strongest application—while also serving to reinforce a psychological connection to the narrative.

Two different size pieces (2" x 4" and 4" x 4") of end grain slabs were laid out interspersed with each other, creating enough disturbance in the visual field to visually register the material.

"When we first started designing the wine walls surrounding the stair, it seemed like we were heading for danger. Despite a decision to not temperature or humidity condition the wine, these glass vitrines were designed as simply as possible but still constituted a hurdle with a lot of moving parts and very little time to actually build. Fortunately, our crack team of steelworkers from Chinatown parked themselves on site, and had the guidance of legends Johnny Li Sr. and Johnny Li Jr. to help shed light on the subject. Senior especially did a beautiful job converting our construction drawings into his own axon sketches (see below), translating our sloppy English into clearer to understand Chinese. What should have taken months to build was completed in two weeks."

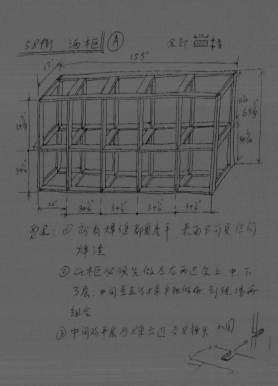

WOOD ENVELOPE

Fascinated by traditional wooden meat lockers, cold rooms, and ice boxes from the turn of the century (and inspired by one we found on site behind one of the demolished walls), an exploration began into these early means of refrigeration. Although a meat locker doesn't exactly conjure up images of fine dining, we were mostly interested in the aesthetics of its construction and the sensory experience of being completely enveloped in a singular material.

SCREWED

A meat locker from the early twentieth century would have had an interior construction that was sheathed in tin, and then covered with tongue-and-groove wood planks securely hammered in with nails. The thing that was always so striking about photos of early meat lockers was the precision with which the boards were nailed, and the serendipitous pattern of nail heads that such attention to detail had produced. In contextualizing this inherent artistry, we designed a system of tongue-and-groove wood planks specifying the exact placement of stainless steel tamper proof screws; an homage to the ideals of craftsmanship evident in these photos and yet so rarely practiced today. The screw pattern adds a strong graphic presence, and required over ten thousand screws (and an extremely patient carpenter) to pull off.

"The contractor bought New York, New Jersey, and Connecticut completely out of this particular screw. Construction was actually held up in this area until more screws could be located, we think from somewhere in Nebraska? 2 1/4-inch-long #7 small countersunk, trim head, square drive, stainless steel wood screws....what's so hard to find?"

Tuesday Feb 22ᵈ 1853

Stephen S. Westcott Dr Self
6 Yds Bleached   1/3   94
2 "   Linen   5/6   1.37
2 doz Buttons   6   13
2 Spools   5ᵈ   11
Cards & Note Paper 5/6   69
1 Silk Hat   24/-   3 11
1 pr Kid Gloves   7/-   87   7.

Raymond L. Wright Dr
1 ply Stripe Shirting 1/-

MARKET GREENS

Floral and organic additions in any project are important and are considered carefully. For Quality Meats we wanted to stay pared down, raw, and more vegetal than floral. At first this wasn't met with open arms (big bloomy flowers being as popular as they are in midtown), but we knew it could be pulled off, look great, and be more consistent with the concept of the space.

"To ensure the fresh 'market' aesthetic, we sourced elegant looking vegetables like anise, swiss chard, and scallions from a variety of local stores and discussed whether we could have a go at making them into rotating installations, integrated as a complete part of the architecture. We decided it could be achieved if we added separate supermarket runs to the florist's weekly change outs, along with a specification list exacting which additional vegetables to buy. Essentially, we had her running round to every small market in the neighborhood to find our 'specified' goods until she made a well-founded complaint and we had to ease up on our restrictions."

OPEN SESAME

The steel and glass partition at the south end of the second floor dining room was designed to appear like a permanent wall, bordering the space with back lit austerity and maintaining a certain level of intimacy in the space. However, this partition folds and pivots into four panels, giving the flexibility of opening up another equally sized dining space to be used for additional seating on busy evenings or kept closed to contain the additional room as a private event space.

HOOKED

Oftentimes inspiration will appear in the most unexpected places. A photograph showing clusters of meat hooks and trolleys interlinked in a meatpacking facility in New York resonated immediately with us. The somewhat dangerous character of the meat hook was transcended by the fact that its function was turned to performing less dastardly tasks. The tight, linear grouping of the objects and the intricacy of their design also had an organic quality that struck us, similar to the display of fowl hanging from a shop window. The absurdity that these otherwise dangerous looking objects could have such a delicacy about them in both appearance and function was too much to pass up.

An amalgam of tongs, hooks and wheeled trolleys became the vehicle with which to deliver light to long stretches of tables at Quality Meats; each part of the assembly was nickel plated in order to remove its typically industrial connotation and re-present it in a new light. Like chandeliers from a twisted butcher cum welder's workshop, these completely custom fixtures ran along a blackened steel I-beam on wheeled hangers. Each light could be moved along the beam to hover over any combination of tables as required by the flexibly seated banquette below.

"We had the idea for this light fixture near the beginning of the project, and made a number of sketches of it, even going so far as to put renditions of them into early elevations. But frankly, we weren't sure what it actually was or how to make it, and with so many other more pressing matters constantly at hand, we put the drawing in our back pocket and figured we'd get to them later. It wasn't until the end of the project that we finally ordered a bunch of parts and built a prototype over a weekend. We still remember showing up the following Monday with a smile on our faces as if we had had it sorted the entire time."

DINNER SHOULD BE DANGEROUS
(FROM TIME TO TIME)

One of the principles we often put into practice is that of imparting a function to typically decorative items, representing them with new purpose. In the private upstairs dining room, we decided to exercise the opposite tack by taking an object of utility—in this case, the quintessential butcher's tool, the meat cleaver—and rendering it useless by transforming it into an object of ornament. Referencing a scene more often found in the back room of a meatpacking plant than a fine dining restaurant, the resulting installation is visually arresting, a little bit humorous, and somewhat unsettling.

"We scoured antique stores to find these vintage cleavers, most of them about to be discarded simply because the owner just didn't know what to do with them. Each one we found was unique, from the detailing of the handles to the shape of the blade and the branding of the manufacturer, and some even looked homemade. What we loved best about them was that they showed obvious signs of history—the wood handles developed a beautiful patina from years of use, the blades rusted and corroded, interesting textures and colors of a fading art."

PHONE ROOM

Since the majority of Quality Meats' interior occurs either below grade or far from a direct visual connection to the outside, cellular service throughout the restaurant is less than ideal. In homage to a pre-cell phone era when payphones were located in every restaurant near its restrooms, we took an unused storage room in the basement near the Men's and Lady's and created an old-school, lush telephone lounge. A bronze bull's head mounted on felt damask wallpaper watches over leather armchairs and an antique rotary phone. Local calls are free.

A COMMON LOO

The restrooms in the basement at Quality Meats were designed as tongue-in-cheek derivations of the type of attended wash rooms often found in New York. The idea of putting expensive objects, finishes, and employees into the most pedestrian of environments to insinuate the idea of "high class" is a notion we attempted to bring to a more "common" level.

Large expensive slabs of marble are substituted by economical off cuts (1" x 1" white Carerra marble tiles), slightly mismatched porcelain pedestal sinks replace the austerity of earlier versions, and hundreds of pre-folded linen towels sit lining an entire wall (empty but useful tools of a wash room attendant who never comes). Antique brass soap dishes and toothbrush holders have been repurposed to perform as candleholders interspersed throughout the space—votive candles fit so well in these that many people believe that this was their original function.

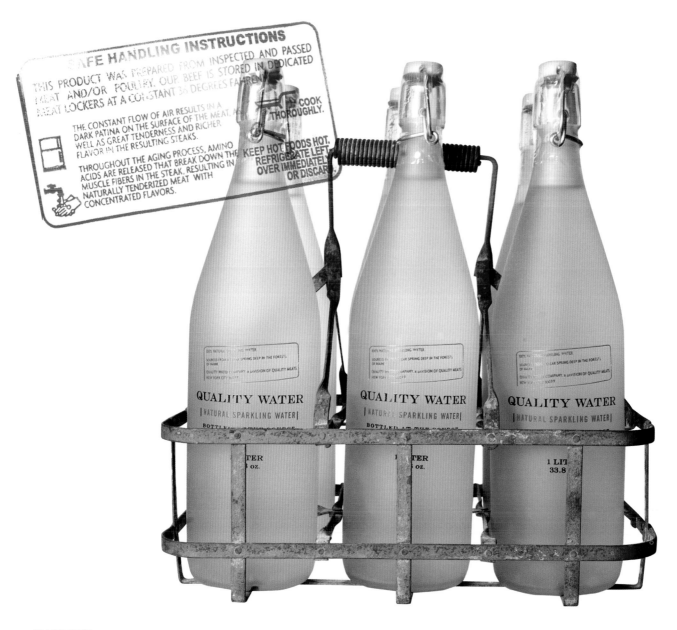

IDENTITY

For the identity of Quality Meats we sought to bridge the gap between classic butcher shop sensibilities and modern meat packaging iconography. A timeless Engravers font harkens back to a time when simple readability was tantamount. This was often seen on posters, playbills, newspapers, and similarly interpreted for shop signage. Marrying this style with a more contemporary graphic language speaks to the nature of the restaurant itself. Icons from the lexicon of consumerism and meat purchasing/preparation find their way into the mix via a USDA stamp style application often found on many packaged meats. The "safe handling instructions" root the identity in the butcher shop/grocery mentality and keep the product close to its source of origin. These "handling instructions" are modified for various purposes and applications: food, wine and water bottles. Each stamp has content that is not only slightly cheeky, but accurate and informative for the product it labels.

SAFE HANDLING INSTRUCTIONS

THIS PRODUCT WAS PREPARED FROM INSPECTED AND PASSED MEAT AND/OR POULTRY. OUR BEEF IS STORED IN DEDICATED STEAK LOCKERS AT A CONSTANT ___ DEGREES FAHRENHEIT.

THE CONSTANT FLOW OF AIR RESULTS IN A DARK PATINA ON THE SURFACE OF THE MEAT AS WELL AS GREAT TENDERNESS AND RICHER FLAVOR IN THE RESULTING STEAKS.

THROUGHOUT THE AGING PROCESS, AMINO ACIDS ARE RELEASED THAT BREAK DOWN THE MUSCLE FIBERS IN THE STEAK, RESULTING IN NATURALLY TENDERIZED MEAT WITH CONCENTRATED FLAVORS.

COOK THOROUGHLY.

KEEP HOT FOODS HOT. REFRIGERATE LEFT-OVER IMMEDIATELY OR DISCARD.

QUALITY MEATS

57 W 58TH ST NEW YORK, NEW YORK 10019

www.qualitymeatsnyc.com

WEIGHED | SELL BY

T: 212-371-7777 | F: 212-371-9362

06

PAST IMPERFECT

RAYMOND NADEAU

"This world, the eternally imperfect, an eternal contradiction's image and imperfect image—an intoxicating joy to its imperfect creator—thus did the world once seem to me."

—Friedrich Nietzche, Thus Spake Zarathustra

At the beginning of this book the notion of "best ugly" was introduced as an acquired model of aesthetic appreciation. Past imperfect, its grammatical foil, designates a past tense verb, suggesting an incomplete action or condition. Continuity is implied and completion of an action is frequently linked with another action that has yet to be determined. For many of us, the past imperfect tense is merely an annoying complication of grammatical artifice; it sounds slippery. It is the tense reserved for lawyers and lovers.

For the truly brave of heart, however, the notions of best ugly and past imperfect can represent keys, unlocking the doors of physics and even the multiple dimensions of time. They allow for inexplicable cultural quirks, iconography, and human emotion to enter into the often cold languages of pure design, pure science, or pure anything. Nothing in reality is pure. Design finds its human voice via the past imperfect tense—allowing it to challenge and/or recreate the very notions of what is real, has been real, and could be real. The language of the divine has always been spoken in the past imperfect tense. Had man remained true to his creator, or his essential being, the world would have been a far different place. There is the suggestion of perfection—without the literal presence of perfection. Herein lies the past and present danger.

If you believe in heresy, AvroKO might be branded heretical. Its visual, contextual, and psychological design always speaks in the past imperfect tense, the divine tense, hitting upon not only the notion of best ugly, but also upon any number of chaos-compliant, humanist concessions—that is, imperfect perfections. Every design statement seems perfectly incomplete, as though it requires the insertion of an "actor" to complete the "occupation" of design. The actor, or anyone entering one of AvroKO's designed spaces, is naturally compelled to act out the passion plays set in motion through design, but without a complete choreography or script.

Improvisational stories set in AvroKO's environments bring design to life and allow for the dynamic tension that differentiates a human drama from a morality play. Any meaning that results is spontaneous, more akin to an oral tradition of storytelling than to an overly researched recreation of a fictional past. Any interaction is real and immediate, heightening the significance of everyday life. Once again, rather than precisely framing what was or explaining what is, the past imperfect tense suggests the conditions and actions that point to what might be, or perhaps what should have been had we the luxury of rewriting history.

An artist must experience the world around him (ugly or not) lest his or her art lose touch with life—transitioning into a dead language of sorts, like ancient Greek or Latin. A new enlightenment is at hand. Our convictions and places within the new creative universe are shifting as we transition from a spectator to a participatory culture. The obligation of architecture, design, and all art forms is to lift those disciplines to a place where cultural relevance and, more importantly, a sense of shared cultural meaning are achieved. For living is and always has been the ultimate art. When we accept this, we also allow for the fact that perhaps the truest art can't be seen at all. Which brings us back to AvroKO's emphasis on experience and design connectivity.

The ultimate question here is whether design connectivity makes the world a better place. Does life become less lonely within a space defined by shared meaning? Does shared meaning contribute to collaborative reality, bringing people closer together? If the answer to these questions is yes, then AvroKO has hit upon a magic formula.

AvroKO constructs such molds, such elusive art. And, in so doing, captures the essence of living design. Design for now. Design too sweet to lose. AvroKO's loose interpretations bring their constructed experiential environments closer to, not further from, reality. AvroKO has discovered the real and celebrates it with passion and compassion. They create both the shadow and the substance of solidly shifting experiential design.

"Nothing in reality is pure. Design finds its human voice via the past imperfect tense—allowing it to challenge and/or recreate the very notions of what is real, has been real, and could be real."

ACKNOWLEDGMENTS

We would like to thank a considerable number of people, including the many friends, colleagues and complete strangers who have come along on our many project adventures.

RESTAURANT PROJECT ACKNOWLEDGMENTS:

A very special thanks to Chris Larkin, who has either managed the construction of, or significantly contributed to, every restaurant project to date. Thanks for staying up all those late nights, offering your skills far away beyond the call of duty, and generally saving us from certain disaster more than a few times.

Thanks to all of our investors in PUBLIC for betting on us early in the game. In addition, thanks to Dan Rafalin and Brad Farmerie, our PUBLIC partners in crime, for joining us on this amazing journey.

Thanks to our clients whose projects are represented over the previous pages. Thank you for hiring us, for putting up with us, and for becoming good friends in the process.

Rich Wolf, Peter Kane, Chris Santos (The Stanton Social)

Brian Matzkow, Joe Levy, Patricia Yeo (Sapa)

Jason Hennings and Bob Giraldi (E.U.)

Robert Ianello, Joe Caruso, Ralph Tramontata, Chris Ianello (Odea)

Alan and Michael Stillman (Quality Meats)

To all of our staff, past and present, who have dedicated themselves entirely to the work. We are extremely honored to work alongside such remarkable talent.

Joe Calabrese	Anne Miller
Mark Castilanni	Asuka Nakao
Tina Chang	Krista Ninivaggi
Wit Chong	Ariana Rinderknecht
Andrew Cohen	Yvette Santiago
Helen Davies	Travis Schnupp
Sam Espada	Neill Seltzer
Kristine Ganancial	Yong Ho Sin
Randi Halpern	Skye Sullivan
Lynn Juang	Ryan Thomas
Jarod Kitchen	Jeff Uptain
Yuki Kuwana	Chris Wigginton
Kadi Lublin	Michi Yanagashita
Norma Marchand	

And also, to the numerous people who helped to bring the construction of these New York restaurant projects to fruition, whose passions for their crafts are truly appreciated.

PUBLIC:

Mikel Abreau, Stuart Goldstein, Linus Ilario, Chris Larkin, Ming Li, Mike Mizell, Yukio Nagashima, Mike Parris, Ted Salmon, Jim Savio, Kurt Schwartzbaum, Patrick Townsend, Alejandro Victoria, Jorge Victoria, Miguel Victoria

THE STANTON SOCIAL:

Maurice Cyms, John Kole, Chris Larkin, Ronnie Lieberman, Matt Lusk, Matteo Massanet, Amir Moghul, Phil Morgan, Ted Salmon, (and all at Hecho, Munrod, and Town & Country)

SAPA:

Joe Colgan, Maurice Cyms, Ray Khan, Chris Larkin, Russ Lawrence, Ming Li, Amir Moghul, Mike Mizell, Mike Parris, Bob Perry, Kurt Schwartzbaum, Fernando Urrea, Jayda Uras, Alejandro Victoria, Miguel Victoria (and all at Munrod, Studio NY, and Source)

EU:

Maurice Cyms, Ray Khan, John Kole, Chris Larkin, Johnny Li (Jr. and Sr.), Barb McCrae, Matteo Massanet, Mike Mizell, Amir Moghul, Phil Morgan, Kurt Schwartzbaum, Bryan Stockdale, Fernando Urrea, Peter Yuan (and all at Hecho, Olde Good Things, and Winsor Fireform)

ODEA:

Stuart Goldstein, Chris Larkin, Amir Moghul, Mike Parris, Bob Perry, Patrick Townsend (and all at Rollhaus and Studio NY)

QUALITY MEATS:

Terry Bovill, Joe Colgan, Terry Cummings, Jerry Devine, Eamon Gilroy, Dale Jacobs, Ray Khan, Chris Larkin, Johnny Li (Jr. and Sr.), Segal Liviu, Dennis Martin, Mike Mizell

BOOK ACKNOWLEDGMENTS:

Judith Regan, for both generously supporting us through this process and pushing us to create a better product. Also, many thanks to Anna Bliss, Matt Cacciola and Richard Ljoenes at HarperCollins for their unswerving patience and guidance.

Michael Weber, who has spent countless three AM photo shoots to produce the majority of our beautiful architecture shots.

Travis Schnupp, who brought his superb graphic talents to the look and feel of this book.

Yuki Kuwana, who has essentially made this book possible through her skillful and obsessive photography of details in each restaurant.

Lynn Juang, who helped bring intelligent thought to the content and organization of this book during the lengthy process of putting it all together.

Jon Crawford-Phillips, for subjecting himself to hours and hours of cocktails, on countless evenings, in order to pen his overarching introduction essay and to bring order to our rowdy interviews.

Alia Akkam, Kristi Cameron, Jay Cheshes, Olga Katsnelson, Jen Renzi, and Andrea Strong for their amazing essays in this book as well as the stellar writing they have done on our projects over the years. One million thank-yous for their time and enthusiastic energy.

Raymond Nadeau, for championing us from the beginning and sharing his brilliant thoughts in his closing essay.